Fig. 1.

Craftsmen and Cabinet-makers of
Classic English Furniture

Craftsmen and Cabinet-makers of
Classic English Furniture
Geoffrey Wills

ST. MARTIN'S PRESS   NEW YORK

Printed in Great Britain
Library of Congress Catalog Card Number: 75–34773
First published in the United States of America in 1976

Library of Congress Cataloging in Publication Data

Wills, Geoffrey.
    Craftsmen and cabinet-makers of classic English furniture.
    Bibliography: p.
    Includes index.
    1. Furniture industry and trade—Great Britain—
History. 2. Furniture, English. I. Title.

TS810.G7W54 1976 749.2'2 75–34773

Contents

ACKNOWLEDGMENTS

The following black and white illustrations are from
Ambrose Heal, LONDON FURNITURE MAKERS,
Batsford, 1953:
Numbers: 70, 82, 83, 85, 86, 88, 89, 95, 96 and 112.

NOV 9   1976

Illustrations

Black and White Illustrations: those marked with an asterisk are line-drawings by Richard Roe.

Introduction

There have always been collectors of old English furniture, and during the present century much time has been devoted to its study. More recently, interest has begun to be shown in the men who made it and the methods they employed. The French eighteenth-century custom of a cabinet-maker putting his name to his work by means of a metal stamp was only rarely followed in England, where there existed instead the occasional habit of sticking a printed paper label on a piece. Many of these flimsy 'signatures' have vanished with the passing of the years, but quite a number have been recorded and more will doubtless come to light in the future. In the following pages there is a brief history of furniture styles between about 1550 and 1850, followed by a discussion of some of the more important cabinet-makers, their business methods and the articles they produced.

G.W.

Furniture 1550-1720

Very little furniture has survived from the years before 1550, and what remains shows nothing more than simple workmanship. This may be due to the fact that only heavily-constructed pieces have been able to withstand the ravages of time. The comparatively elegant articles disappeared long ago, and are known to us only from illustrations in manuscripts.

The majority of surviving pieces are chests, which were deliberately made in a substantial manner in order to protect their contents. They were convenient repositories for documents and valuables, and it was intended that they should be as thiefproof as possible. The thickness of their timbers deterred the armoury and skill of a potential miscreant, while the weight of the chest made removal a difficult or impossible matter.

Among the earlier examples, current during the Middle Ages and not easy to date precisely, are those constructed from a length of tree-trunk in which a cavity has been hacked. A lid was formed from a piece previously cut from the log and then hinged and reinforced with iron bands. Such 'dug out' chests required only the most elementary tools for their making and, indeed, in the years when they were produced only the simplest implements were available.

The construction of chests in the thirteenth century shows a considerable advance on the foregoing method. At that time flat planks of wood were being employed and both the mortice and tenon joints and dowel fixings had been adopted. The tenon is a simple method of joining by placing a tongue of one piece of wood into a slot formed in another, the whole being held firmly together with a wooden pin or dowel driven into a hole made through mortice and tenon.

The planks themselves were usually of oak, a wood which lent itself particularly well to their production. The timber of the tree has a straight grain that allows it to be split lengthwise without too much difficulty, and boards were obtained by driving wedges into the ends of logs. The boards having been riven radially, they were narrower towards the centre of the trunk, and were also limited in width to half the diameter of the latter. It was a far easier method than cutting planks out with a saw, which explains why so much of the earlier furniture was made from oak. Elm, for instance, could not be riven owing to its different type of grain, and could only be made into planks by laboriously sawing it.

The saw had been known to man since Prehistoric times and was commonly used by the Romans. When the Empire of the latter collapsed and was succeeded by the Dark Ages, the saw and much else was forgotten. Eventually it was re-invented, depending on the progress of improvements in metal-making for its gradual development. Large baulks of timber were sawn by teams of men standing above and below the timber, pulling and pushing the saw in turn. By this means flat planks were produced, in contrast to the irregular riven ones, and as they could be taken from the full width of the trunk they were consequently of much greater breadth.

The tasks of trimming off the bark and smoothing the surfaces of a plank were performed by means of axes and adzes. The former remains in use after a service to mankind stretching back into pre-history, with no sign of it ever becoming redundant. The adze, however, is now seldom seen, although in its day it was an important tool. It comprises a metal blade with a sharp edge, somewhat akin to an axe but with the handle placed at right-angles instead of parallel to the curved blade. The tool is

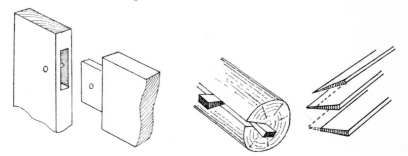

1   Mortice and tenon.

2   Oak log riven with wedges, and planks.

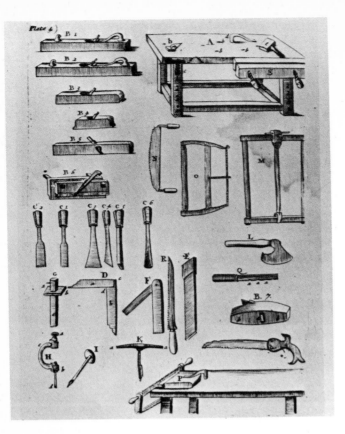

3 Carpenters' tools and benches, from Moxon's *Mechanick Exercises*, published in 1678.

used with a swinging motion so that it 'hooks' away inequalities, and in skilful hands could, and still can, produce a smooth finish.

Further and even finer finishing required a plane, a tool of almost equally lengthy ancestry to the afore-mentioned, and one which has changed little in appearance over the centuries. A variation of it was used in making mouldings and grooves; the blade and sole, or base, of the plane being shaped according to requirements.

The spread of learning in the mid-sixteenth century led to demands for more sophisticated furnishings and to improvements in wood-working methods. The principal change was to replace the simple board with a number of smaller framed pieces of flat wood. This successfully disguised the effects of natural shrinkage as timber aged, and at the same time enabled larger surfaces, such as the walls of rooms, to be covered in an attractive manner.

It was achieved by making panels: small-sized thin rectangles of oak framed within thicker horizontal and vertical pieces. The thin members could expand and shrink without hindrance as they fitted only loosely, cracks were avoided and the whole structure was strong and durable. In addition, less timber was required, and with no necessity for pieces of large area costs were kept down and finished articles were lighter in weight. Although panelling of this kind was used for lining the walls of rooms, it was equally serviceable on a smaller scale for making furniture. Chests could be constructed, or 'joined' in this manner, but it was adaptable also to other articles. Its making called for more skill than that of the average carpenter, and before long those who did the work were known as joiners.

In 1571 a charter was granted to the London Company of Joiners and Ceilers; the latter being the name for those specialising in wall-panelling, although it has been argued that ceilers were carvers. The subjects of Queen Elizabeth I demanded that their better woodwork should be ornamented in as fine a style as possible, and while much of it was painted and gilded, a variety of carving was in use. The undermentioned were employed either singly or in combination (see Figs. 8–11, page 20):

Chip-carving: facets cut away to form rosettes and other simple shapes. A popular form of ornament from medieval times down to the mid-seventeenth century and occasionally later.

Sunk carving: patterns remaining after the surrounding wood is cut away, and with the ground left flat or given a matt surface by means of a metal punch or a nail.

Incised carving: designs made by cutting shallow lines.

Gouging: commonly seen in the shape of rows of arcading. Produced by a round bladed chisel which makes a curved furrow.

There was also an increasing employment of inlay, for which pieces of wood of contrasting colour were inset so as to form patterns. This was a variation of sunk carving, by which the recesses were carefully made and the inlays fitted into them somewhat in the manner of a jig-saw puzzle.

Parallel with the joiner's craft was that of the turner, who made use of a lathe for the manufacture of legs for chairs, stools and tables, and other items such as bed-posts. Members of the Company of Turners were employed traditionally in making wooden domestic

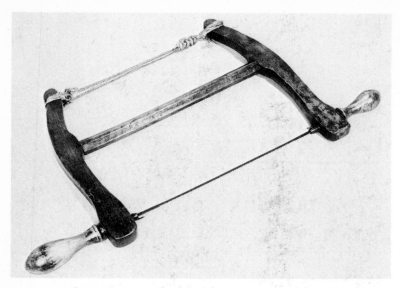

wares and measures, but with a more widespread use of seat furniture they began to embrace that also. In the course of the seventeenth century a chair became the product of four distinct crafts: turning, for the legs and connecting stretchers; joining, for the main frame; carving, for such work with a chisel that was required; and upholstering, for stuffing and covering the seat and back, and the arms, too, if it was an armchair.

Surviving tables of the Elizabethan period can be divided into two categories: those with simple tops, and those with tops that might be expanded in length by withdrawing leaves concealed at each end. These last, which came into fashion in about 1550, replaced or supplemented an earlier variety of table having a rectangular frame with a top composed of planks held together by cross-pieces at the ends. The top was not fixed to the base, so the entire table could be removed in two parts without much difficulty; an important matter at the conclusion of a banquet when floor space was required for revelry. Subsequently, with a room set aside exclusively for dining, there was no need to make the table portable, and the withdrawing type, although the top and leaves could be easily lifted from the frame, was unlikely to be disturbed at the conclusion of a meal. The majority of withdrawing tables average six feet or so in length, whereas some of their predecessors run to four or five times as much.

Noticeable features of the tables dating from about 1600 are their legs, which take the form of large turnings elaborately carved with acanthus leaves and ribs. In the case of the more decorative examples, each leg is headed

Plate 1 Armchair decorated in the Chinese manner on a red ground, by Giles Grendey (1693–1780). Height 113cm.

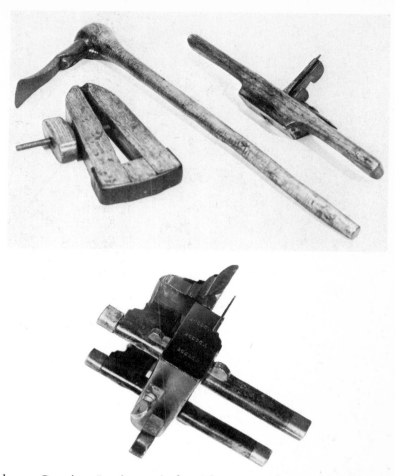

5 (Centre) adze with a naturally grown handle; (left) oak clamp with leather hinge; (right) spokeshave. All 19th century.

6 Moulding plane, the name on the front is that of a former owner. Elsewhere it is stamped with the name of the maker, W. Greenslade, who was active in Bristol from the mid-19th century. Length 21·5cm.

Plate 2 Carved giltwood armchair made by Thomas Chippendale to a design by Robert Adam, 1764.

by a Grecian Ionic capital, with a carved or inlaid frieze resting on its curled volutes.

The rising standard of living of the sixteenth century led to a greatly increased demand for metalwork, especially of iron. To meet this, the iron-masters expanded their production and in so doing were found to be consuming as fuel a dangerously high proportion of the available timber. The quantity of such material was plentiful but not inexhaustible, and the depletion of forests took time to make good. The uses of wood extended not only to the making of furniture and as fuel for industry and the home but, of paramount importance, to ship-building. At a time when the country was threatened by the armada of Philip of Spain, it was considered essential to protect this vital resource.

In 1557 an Act of Parliament prohibited the cutting of timber in specified areas, and in 1584 there was a prohibition on the establishment of further ironworks in Surrey, Kent and Sussex. Coal was tried as an alternative

7 Oak panel
construction.

8 Chip carving.

9 Sunk carving.

10 Incised carving.

11 Gouged carving.

source of heat for the furnaces, and in due course successful results were achieved with it. Hand-operated bellows had earlier provided the draught of air necessary to increase the heat of the flame and remove the maximum of carbon, so that the result was a malleable product rather than brittle cast iron. The adoption of water power increased both the actual quantity of air and its pressure as well as assuring a greater regularity of supply, so that a much improved metal was produced.

One of the effects of the availability of better iron was to permit the manufacture of superior tools. Carving chisels, for instance, could be given a greater degree of sharpness which they retained over a longer period, and the same applied to axes and other cutting implements. It not only led to the introduction of more efficient versions of existing tools, but encouraged the development of improved types. Hitherto each craftsman had had little alternative to making for himself whatever tools he required, calling on the blacksmith to supply the necessary cutting edges and providing his own handles for chisels, stocks for planes, and so forth. Towards the later seventeenth century a change began to take place, and the forerunner of the modern tool manufacturer appeared. He made tools that were completely ready for use, and the joiner was then able to concentrate on furniture-making. Many of the suppliers of tools limited their output to one particular article, such as planes or saws, but in the course of time such distinctions tended to disappear and a single name would appear on a wide range of products.

Advances in metallurgy were not the only factors to affect the making of furniture. The strongest influences were changes in fashion, which led the public to demand different furnishings and inspired craftsmen to supply them. Fashion itself owed its changes apparently to unaccountable whims, but at the time there could have been political and economic factors that defy research and analysis by later students.

The course of the seventeenth century saw quite a number of changes in the design of furniture, the most obvious being an increasing lightness in both weight and appearance, and the widespread use of the drawer. The straightforward chest with its opening on the top was inconvenient when removing anything placed at the bottom of it since all the upper contents had to be taken out before it could be reached. The comparatively shallow drawer provided a satisfactory solution to the problem, and once its advantages became appreciated it could not fail to be popular. It had been used occasionally in the sixteenth century and possibly even earlier, but it was not until about 1650 that drawers were fitted regularly in tables.

A drawer was also fitted sometimes in the base of a chest, lessening the depth of the upper portion and making the piece of furniture more serviceable. In due course, around about 1670, the top opening of the chest was in some cases dispensed with altogether, successive ranges of drawers were fitted in its place and the familiar chest-of-drawers came into being.

The earlier drawers were each made with a deep groove at either side, which corresponded with a raised runner within the opening in the main framework. The drawer was thus suspended at each side, although as the front was made perfectly rectangular there was no external sign of this when it was closed. The back, sides and other parts of these drawers were fixed together in a simple manner with nails. The sides and back were butted one against the other, while the front ends of the sides were either fitted into grooves made to receive them or were inset, in either instance no join being visible at the front. Soon, the grooved drawer was superseded by the type remaining in use today, with flat runners on which the lower edges of its sides can slide.

Alternatively, the dovetail was employed, and with continuing improvements to its efficiency it gradually replaced all other methods of drawer-making. As its name implies, the dovetail bears a resemblance to that part of the bird, or it can be equally described as 'fan-shaped'. The dovetail is cut into one piece of wood and is made to fit tightly into a shaped slot formed in the other piece (see Fig. 51, page 61). The result is a neat, strong and long-lasting joint, which in its fully developed form remains unequalled for its purpose.

The seventeenth century saw also the prominent feature of Tudor times, the massive bulbous support, acquiring simplicity and becoming more slender as the years advanced. Carving was employed less frequently as a decorative element and many pieces of furniture were much plainer than in the past, although applied ornament enjoyed popularity. This took the form of turnings split lengthwise and faceted shapes resembling cut stones. It has been suggested that restrained ornament, or none, was due to the Puritan influence of Oliver Cromwell's rule, and with the nation engaged in civil

12   Turner at work at a treadle lathe; an engraving published in 1763.

13   Turner at work at a pole lathe; an engraving published in 1763.

Fig. 1.

23

strife such details were understandably treated as trivial. In those unsettled times, the majority of Britons made do with the furniture they already possessed, or else they purchased what was a forerunner of the Utility furniture of the 1939–45 war years. Anyone wanting better things made purchases on the Continent and in due course they reached these shores. John Evelyn, the diarist made a note in June 1652 which showed that cross-Channel trade was carried on despite a current quarrel with the Dutch. He recorded that the ship carrying his wife home had managed to pass through the Dutch fleet, which mistook it for a fishing-vessel. In addition to its human cargo it carried seventeen bales of furniture 'which', he wrote, 'I bless God came all safe to land, together with my wife, and my Lady Browne her mother, who accompanied her'. Furnishings came in this way not only from Holland and other areas of the Low Countries, but from farther afield.

With the restoration of a monarchy and the crowning of Charles II in 1660, a big change took place within the space of a few years. Charles had lived abroad for most of the time following the execution of his father in 1649, and he had had an opportunity to see much of foreigners and their homes. Soon after settling in London he married the Portugese, Catherine of Braganza, and to his own taste was added that of his Queen. Additionally, it was not long before the greedy demands of the King's mistresses encouraged the spending of large sums of money on hitherto unheard-of luxuries in the way of furnishing.

Not only did the Continental pieces familiar to Charles look different from those being made in England, but they varied in construction and finish because of changes introduced during the recent decades of comparative isolation. Also, in the train of Charles came a number of craftsmen, principally from Holland but some from other lands, who settled themselves in business in London. They brought with them new designs and techniques, which were quickly imitated and modified where necessary by the established English workers.

The most notable introduction in furniture-making at the time was the use of veneers in place of solid wood. A veneer, a thinly-cut slice of timber usually selected for its interesting markings, was glued to a more commonplace wood backing. It thus made the best possible use of the rarer and costlier material and resulted in a considerably enhanced article. Many striking woods

14 Walnut chair with turned front legs, about 1615. Height 91·5cm.

15 Oak dining table with plank top, turned legs and a gouged frieze, about 1600. Length 3·05m.

16 Oak dining table with withdrawing leaves at each end, about 1600. Length 2·21m.

were employed in this way, and among them was, the most popular then as now, walnut. More expensive and scarce imported woods included kingwood, known at the time as prince's wood or princewood, ebony and amboyna, the latter from the East Indies and remarkable for its close patterning of tiny curls.

Veneering was executed by carefully preparing the surface and scoring it with a series of closely placed lines to afford a good grip for the adhesive, and then gluing in place the thin sheet of walnut or other wood. Its effectiveness was often increased by arranging two or more pieces, cut successively from the same log, so that the resulting design was balanced in its markings. The production of these halved or quartered patterns was not only decorative, but was technically advantageous; it would usually be impossible to obtain a single sheet of veneer of sufficient size to cover a large surface. Also, some of the more striking markings were the result of freaks of growth that weakened the timber and made it unusable unless supported in some way; burr wood, with its pattern of curls, is an example.

Flat areas, such as drawer fronts and the slopes of bureaux, were usually framed by a narrow inner double border of veneer, placed so that the grain was angled in opposing directions to form a herring-bone design. At the extreme edge, with or without the herring-bone, there was frequently a strip of cross-banding: a straight-grained veneer placed so that the grain ran at right angles to the edge (Fig. 20).

Kingwood and laburnum, in particular, which can show striking grain and colour contrasts, were sometimes veneered in the form of slices cut from branches of the parent tree. They produced roughly circular pieces three to four inches in diameter which were arranged to cover the doors of cabinets, drawer-fronts and other suitable surfaces. Because of their likeness to oyster shells they are often referred to as 'oyster' veneers.

Marquetry, with two or more woods cut to form a pattern, was also introduced and proved highly to the liking of the public. The sheets of different veneers were placed on top of one another and cut through with a fine saw, in the manner of fretwork, to the desired pattern. Separated, they formed a perfect fit with each other and could then be glued in place. The various cut sheets would cover more than one surface, as the surplus from each set could all be assembled to make similar patterns although in different contrasts. Thus, veneers of dark- and light-coloured woods could be arranged to form a light-on-dark design and another of dark-on-light. Floral designs were especially favoured, with the leaves sometimes dyed green and shaded for greater realism. John Evelyn, who lived at the time and probably saw the work performed, described the latter as follows:

> When they would imitate the natural turning of leaves . . . they effect it by dipping the pieces so far into hot sand as they would have the shadow.

As the craftsmen grew more skilled at their work they made it more detailed. The so-called 'seaweed' or 'endive' marquetry was the ultimate in this type of veneering. The fine scrolling lines were most often cut in light-coloured holly or box wood to contrast against a background of darker walnut, and careful smoothing resulted in an almost unbroken surface. After three centuries, however, time has formed an outline of fine black lines

17 Detail of a carved oak table leg of about 1600.

18 Late 17th-century chest of drawers with panelled front and sides, the drawers running in grooves. Width 99cm.

26

round the separate pieces, woods have faded and varnish has darkened, so the effect is now different. Although there are a few exceptional instances of cabinets, in which the interiors have been protected from light and dust, appearing as they did when they were made.

The twenty or so years during which elaborate marquetry was fashionable were followed by a period of restrained ornament. Not only was the colourful and lively marquetry superseded by plain but carefully-

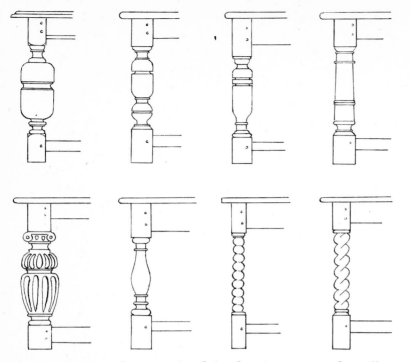

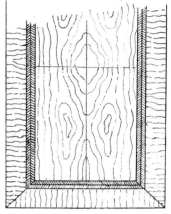

19 Turned table legs from about 1600 to 1680; those on the left are the earliest.

20 Quartered veneer with a border of herring-bone within cross-banding.

chosen veneers, but much of the furniture was of smaller size than hitherto. There may well have been a considerable quantity of earlier articles less bulky than the majority of surviving examples, but little evidence now remains of them. On the other hand, the later Queen Anne walnut specimens are represented by neat tables, bureaux and other pieces which are English adaptations of Dutch originals. They have proved adaptable as regards use, ever-attractive in appearance and look almost as well in a modern setting as they did in the houses in which they were first placed. Of all English antique furniture 'Queen Anne Walnut', Anglo-Dutch in conception, has probably been the inspiration of the greatest number of twentieth century reproductions.

A feature of some pieces made during the reign of Queen Anne, and those made in the succeeding reign of George I, was the revival of carving. It was executed with much greater skill than in earlier times; better tools and the employment of walnut, which was more amenable than oak to such ornament, aiding the craftsman. Chairs and tables particularly benefited from the change, and the well-proportioned cabriole leg with its carved knee and foot is an excellent example of the best workmanship of the day.

Changes in social habits had their effect on the shapes and sizes of pieces of furniture. The large rectangular dining-tables which were a feature of the Tudor hall declined from favour in the course of the seventeenth century, and were replaced by oval-topped tables. At the same time it became the custom for an assembly of persons to dine at a number of small tables rather than, as before, all seated about a single one. The tables, with round or oval tops, were mostly made of oak, with turned supports of the gate-leg type. They included legs to swing out and support the hinged sides of the top, and which tucked away unobtrusively to let down the sides when the table was not required for meals.

By about 1730 tables of similar sizes were being made in mahogany; a stronger wood enabling a less compli-cated support to be used, so that the criss-cross of stretchers linking the legs was no longer needed. The favoured arrangement was for two of the four legs to swing out as before, but without any links at the feet. The members hinging the tops of the legs to the main frame were of oak, and such tables remain a long-lasting

21 Chest of drawers on stand veneered with kingwood 'oysters' and cross-banded, about 1720. Width 1·015m.

tribute to those who evolved the design. Later came the so-called 'spider' tables, with their delicate turned supports. They were strong and at the same time light in weight, and took every advantage of the properties of the wood and the maker's skill.

A further surface decoration for furniture originated in the Far East. In China and Japan wooden articles had for many centuries been given a surface finish of lacquer: the sap of a tree applied in thin coatings, each of which was allowed to dry before the next was put on, and finally given a high polish. The resulting enamel-like surface was then decorated in relief, using colours and gold, or incised and coloured in the grooves, so that the finished product was as attractive as it was durable. Lacquered furniture had been imported into Europe since the late sixteenth century, but 100 years later the trickle of goods became a flood.

By 1700 so much of the furniture was being brought into England from the Orient that there were complaints from British joiners that their employment was jeopardised. They stated that English merchants were sending workmen and models to China, so that the Chinese would be assisted in supplying goods more suitable to the Western market than they had so far found possible. This was, however, possibly a complaint from a minority, as Europeans had already found a way of fighting the competition. This they did by devising imitation lacquers composed of various kinds of varnishes, which bore a superficial resemblance to the original material while lacking most of its good qualities. Additionally, as though to increase the deception, some of the Western-made articles were of Oriental form; for example, rectangular cabinets with folding doors concealing sets of drawers.

To distinguish the Eastern product from its numerous copies the workmanship of the latter is usually termed japanning, stressing that it is not real lacquer. The work was executed in many European countries and it is not always possible to differentiate between that of one country and another. All that can be decided is whether it is genuinely of the correct period, or whether it is of Eastern or Western origin. The work was performed by both professionals and amateurs, and in 1688 two men, John Stalker and George Parker, published at Oxford a book of copper-plate engravings of suitable designs. It was called *A Treatise of Japanning and Varnishing*, and included in its pages were recipes for grounds of various

22 Table top veneered with walnut inset with panels of floral marquetry, about 1680. Width 94cm.

23 Walnut dressing table on cabriole supports with curled brackets at the knees, about 1715. Width 73·7cm.

24 Bureau veneered with burr walnut, the base with a carved frieze and cabriole legs with lion mask knees and lion paw feet, about 1735. Width 81·3cm.

colours as well as patterns showing Chinese figures and landscapes. These, it may be added, are more European than Oriental in appearance, but were sufficiently convincing to satisfy the craving of the time for anything even remotely resembling the mysterious East and its inhabitants.

Among the Chinese importations were large-sized draught screens, some of them standing as much as nine feet in height and having up to a dozen folds. While some of them were no doubt used for their intended purpose, others were employed in England for making and embellishing locally-made furniture. The surfaces of the screens were painstakingly cut into thin slices and applied in the manner of ordinary wood veneer. It happened frequently that the craftsmen responsible ignored the original pattern, which normally ran the length and height of the screen, and glued down the pieces in a completely haphazard manner. The decoration so produced was colourful and attractive but would not withstand a close inspection. The work was executed mostly with incised lacquer, 'Coromandel' or 'Bantam' work as it was named, and in many instances the resulting confused patterns can only be compared with a child's first attempt at a jig-saw puzzle.

Japanning continued to be practised throughout the eighteenth century and for a couple of decades after. Further, it was revived in the twenties of the present century, when the opportunity was taken to supply an almost insatiable demand for old examples. Plain pieces of furniture, especially country-made grandfather clock cases were japanned in the earlier manner with Chinese-style scenes in gold on grounds of red, blue, green and other colours. They can be very deceptive after nearly half-a-century of wear and tear.

A further popular introduction from the Orient was the use of caning for the seats and backs of chairs. Woven split cane was a complete change from stuffed upholstery, and had the additional advantage of being light in weight. Chairs of the type, both arms and singles, were made in large numbers between about 1670 and 1690, many of them with frames of walnut and others of beech japanned black. The latter, which cost less to buy, were susceptible to attack by woodworm and many thousands must have been ruined in this way over the years. Surviving examples in both walnut and beech have noticeably tall backs and must have demanded a good measure of self-discipline in use if disaster was to be avoided. It is

25 Front leg of a wing armchair: walnut, the knee carved with acanthus leaves and the foot a claw-and-ball. About 1740.

26 Oak folding table with gate-leg supports in the form of tapered and fluted columns, about 1670. Width 78·7cm.

likely that many of them were employed more for display than for comfort, following the example of the French Court where chairs were made specifically for the one need or the other.

The 1660's saw also the spread of a fashion for wall-mirrors. Small-sized ones had been in use for at least a century, but the success of the French in casting large plates of glass and silvering them meant that a supply of large mirrors was available for those who could afford their cost. Late seventeenth-century frames took the form of narrow borders of mirror-glass or of carved and gilt wood, but alternatively there were others composed of fragments of imported lacquer or veneered with exotic woods. Shapes ranged from tall uprights made to be placed on the piers between windows, and more or less square examples designed to hang over a mantel.

Furniture 1720-1851

As early as 1671, in an English book describing America, there is a mention of a timber named 'Mohogeney', and by 1700 some of it was being imported into London from the West Indies. The reddish-brown coloured wood employed by cabinet-makers in the past is divisible into three principal varieties: San Domingo, Cuban and Honduras. The first-named, often called 'Spanish mahogany' because it came from a Spanish possession, was a very hard, close-grained timber that darkened with the passage of time from red to nearly black. Cuban mahogany, also hard, did not blacken with age and was often very finely marked, while the Honduras variety did not reach the British Isles until about 1750. It is softer than the other two, with a marked tendency to fade with age. Although a large proportion of mahogany was straight-grained, it was possible to obtain pieces that were well marked and vied in their effective appearance with walnut.

The reason for a change from walnut as the principal furnishing wood is uncertain, but there would seem to have been more than one. Walnut trees throughout France, the main source of supply, fell victim to an exceptionally severe winter in 1709, and the ensuing scarcity of the timber caused the French government to prohibit its export altogether in 1720. In England, the American variety, Virginia walnut, was brought in as a substitute, but even when augmented with home-grown supplies it gradually lost popularity in the face of mahogany. In addition, imports of this last wood were

Plate 3 Breakfront bookcase veneered with amboyna-wood, probably made by Thomas Wood in 1757. Width 2·44m.

27 Mahogany 'spider' table with gate-leg supports, about 1780. Width 71cm.

Plate 4 Satinwood cabinet with unusual glazing-bars, the base fitted with a drawer and raised on square tapering legs, about 1780. Width 69cm.

encouraged by Parliament, who passed a Bill in 1722 allowing timber from British settlements to enter the country duty free for a period of 21 years. This applied in Jamaica where, it was said, logs from other West Indian sources, not British-owned, mingled with the local product to be labelled collectively 'Jamaican' and so evade payment. Ample supplies of mahogany were soon available and it became preferred to any other wood.

It has been recorded that the first piece of mahogany furniture was made in England for a Dr. Gibbons in 1724. He had been given some planks of the timber by his brother, a West India ship's captain, who had

brought them over as ballast. Dr. Gibbons attempted
to use the wood in a house he was having built in King
Street, Covent Garden, but the carpenters found it too
hard to work. Finally, a local cabinet-maker of the
name of Wollaston made some of the mahogany into a
candle-box 'which outshone in beauty all the doctor's
other furniture'. Dr. William Gibbons is known to have
lived between 1649 and 1728, and a cabinet-maker named
Wollaston had premises in Long Acre in about 1710–20
so there may well be a basis of truth in the story.

While the new timber was made up in forms similar
to those executed until that date in walnut, it was soon
discovered that the two woods had different qualities
demanding separate treatment. Walnut had been
appreciated for its distinctive markings of which the best
use was made in the shape of veneers; flat surfaces being
visually broken-up by their skilful application. The
earlier importations of mahogany, on the other hand,

38

were straight-grained and unsuitable for the same exploitation. Thus, quartered and cross-banded panels were replaced by panels having bevelled (fielded or chamfered) edges held within a frame. It was a return to the earlier way of employing oak (see page 14), but now it was for different reasons. On this occasion it was to please the eye, which was satisfied by the light and shade of mouldings in place of variations in the colour and marking of the wood itself, whereas formerly it was for technical considerations.

The legs of walnut chairs were carved on the knees and feet, and the backs were sometimes of solid wood or, in the better examples, veneered. Mahogany followed suit, except for the veneering which was replaced by carving; this gradually increased in quantity and complexity until it reached a climax in the so-called 'Ribband Back'. The back centred on a simulated bow of ribbon, which taxed not only the strength of the timber but the skill of the carver. Such very elaborate patterns were, however, usually carved from wood glued in layers, the grain in each running in an opposing direction, making it a forerunner of modern machine-made plywood and providing adequate reinforcement without affecting its appearance.

Tables for placing against a wall were to be found in many rooms, mostly made of mahogany but occasionally of walnut. Known at the time as 'Frames', they were in reality little more than supports for their tops, which were invariably the most decorative and valuable parts. Rare marbles were imported from far afield, and some were inlaid with patterns in the manner of wood marquetry in coloured composition or in actual marbles. To the cost of quarrying and working the stone had to be added that of transport, which was usually accomplished by sea in days when roads were poor or almost non-existent. The wooden portion of the tables comprised a rectangular frame on four supports, or on two in the case of console tables, which more or less followed the current patterns of chair legs. The knee was often carved with a stylised scallop shell and a few pendant husks, and the foot was in the form of either an eagle's claw grasping a ball, or the paw of a lion with realistic shaggy hair. In the latter case the frieze centred in a lion mask (Fig. 38).

At about the same date as the change from walnut to mahogany was taking place, in about 1730, there was also a fashion for gilt furniture. This was usually constructed of pine; a soft wood that carved without difficulty and was suitable for finishing with gesso

30 Chinese twelve-fold screen of Coromandel or Bantam incised lacquer, about 1700. Height 2·83m.

31 Walnut armchair with caned seat and back, the latter surmounted by two cupids holding a crown and stamped under the seat-rail with the initials R P. It is probably the mark of Richard Price, a maker of chairs and stools. About 1680. Height 1·168m. (See page 125.)

and gold leaf. The process of gilding was a complex one requiring more skill than is immediately apparent and, unchanged in essentials, remains in use to the present day.

The method consists of coating the carved work with successive layers of the gesso: a mixture of whiting and size. According to an old recipe the size could be made as follows:

> Take two pounds of the cuttings and shavings of clean parchment; the scriveners vend it for 3d. the pound: wash it and put it in a gallon of fair water, boil it to a jelly, then strain and suffer it to cool, and you will find it a strong size.

When the gesso had dried hard, it was rubbed smooth and any of the finer carving that had been obscured was then re-cut. The whole was then painted with a mixture of size and red clay, and on the tacky surface was placed the gold leaf. It was pure gold beaten to less than the thickness of tissue-paper, so careful handling was required to avoid any waste of what has always been a coveted and costly metal.

The foregoing is a brief description of what is known as water-gilding, which can be given a finish by burnishing the raised portions. Rubbing hard with a dog's tooth or a piece of smooth agate results in the burnished parts shining brilliantly against the unpolished matt background.

Alternatively, there was a slightly different process named oil-gilding. It involved the same application of gesso, smoothing and re-cutting, but then came a divergence. In place of water-based size as an adhesive for the gold, a substance made from linseed oil, gold-size, was painted on. Again the gold leaf was laid on top, but as it would not take a polish oil-gilding is entirely matt. As a compensation for its less decorative appearance it is longer-lasting.

To vary the background of carved and gilt work in pine, it was often patterned with tiny circles stamped with a hammer and punch. Alternatively, coarse sand was sprinkled on size or glue and provided an equally interesting contrast with the raised and burnished parts.

Carved and gilt wood was employed successfully for large side-tables and looking-glass frames, both of which were predominant features of a well-furnished room. It was also used on a smaller scale for decorative tables, stands for lacquer cabinets, for candlesticks and

32 Tall looking-glass, the main plate in two portions and the whole bordered by cut and engraved silvered glass within a narrow giltwood frame. About 1710.

candelabra, and for stools and chairs. In many cases it was a fanciful extravagance and the articles could hardly have been expected to withstand normal daily usage. Had they been subjected to much wear and tear during the past 250 years there would be even fewer surviving specimens than there are. As it is, their workmanship has stood up remarkably well to stresses and strains of one kind and another, and with careful treatment there seems no reason to doubt that a proportion will endure for as long again.

Patterns found on giltwood pieces were at first in the Baroque style introduced from the Continent in the late seventeenth century. Typical Baroque features are scrolls and strapwork uniting the various minor elements, and the use of a female mask to provide a focal point. By 1725 this was replaced by the Palladian style founded on the works of the Italian architect, Andrea Palladio, who died in 1580 but whose influence was widespread and long-lasting. The Palladian style as revived in furnishing is recognisable from its use of heavy mouldings such as are usually found round doorways and windows, and a general tendency to weightiness in keeping with the architectural ornament of the time. This is not surprising in view of the fact that for the first time it became the practice for an English designer to plan not only a house, but also the ornamentation and furnishing of its principal rooms.

William Kent, born at Bridlington, Yorkshire, in 1684 was the first to attempt making an entity of a house and its contents. He was a keen student of Palladio's work, combining the role of architect with that of a designer of furniture, a painter of portraits and murals and a planner of gardens. In addition, his less orthodox commissions included the design of a State barge for Frederick, Prince of Wales, the son of George II. Some of Kent's drawings for the vessel still exist and the actual vessel may be seen at the National Maritime Museum, Greenwich, in England. The house-like cabin and its varied ornament in carved and gilt wood show many similarities to Kent's mansions and the tables and chairs he put inside them.

Not all carved pine furniture was gilded at the time it was made, and it is probable that quite a lot was treated at later dates so as to accord with changed taste. Some may have been intended to be left plain, but much was given a coat of flat paint which has long since been renewed or replaced, so that the original appearance can only be surmised. Sometimes gilding was applied to

33 Rectangular looking-glass in a 'cushion' frame of walnut and floral marquetry surmounted by a marquetry and pierced cresting. About 1690. Height 1·143m.

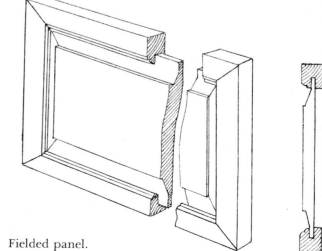

34 Fielded panel.

walnut and mahogany pieces in order to emphasise carving and make the whole article look richer. Partial gilding of this kind, whether carried out on silverware or furniture, being indicated by the term 'parcel gilt'.

A similar effect to the foregoing was achieved by a few makers in about 1740, who followed the French fashion of using gilded bronze mounts in place of carving, gilt or plain. One at least went even further and imitated a Parisian habit of inlaying the wood with strips of brass to form narrow bordering lines, and with larger shaped pieces of brass embellished with engraving (Fig. 43).

In the years 1750–60 carved mahogany furniture was at the very peak of its popularity, and the extravagant and more costly examples resemble the work of a sculptor rather than a wood-carver. By that date the joiner, who had earlier come to the fore as a more skilled type of carpenter, was himself supplanted by one of even greater

35 Walnut chair on cabriole legs with carved knees and claw-and-ball feet. About 1720.

46

competence: the cabinet-maker. He had come to the fore in the early 1700's and in the ensuing decades consolidated the predominance of his position among the various grades of wood-worker.

The style of decoration most employed in the mid-century was known as Rococo; a version of the French word *rocaille*, meaning rock-work. It gained the name because many of the motifs in it were rocks, plants and other natural forms, although many tended to become difficult to recognise after treatment by some of the more advanced designers. A further feature, although not always present, was a deliberate lack of balance between one half of a pattern and the other. Hitherto, the frame of a looking-glass, for instance, had invariably been of precisely matching design at either side, but in its full Rococo form it would be manifestly asymmetrical (Fig. 44). Some of its scrolls on the left might be pointing upwards, while those on the right might be in the reverse direction, producing a studied disorder that is not to every taste.

The public was, as ever, fickle in its likes and dislikes, and the pendulum of style was due for a further swing. Now, it became apparent that carving was no longer to be tolerated, and the chisel was set aside in favour of the tools used for veneering and marquetry. The skills required a century ago and subsequently largely abandoned were put to use again, but no longer to glue down acres of walnut. Fresh woods had been found and were now available to enlarge the scope of workers and designers.

This time a change in tastes involved a return to antiquity, which occurred as a result of intense interest throughout Europe in discoveries made in the ruins of the old Roman cities of Herculaneum and Pompeii. English travellers brought back their own reports of what they had seen there and elsewhere, and the Scottish-born architect, Robert Adam, played an important part in translating the old into the new for the benefit of the British Isles. The style, known as the Neo-classical, was as orderly and prim as the rococo had been wild and free. It employed among other motifs, winged griffins; the anthemion, a floral form resembling a honeysuckle blossom; round and oval discs, paterae; and tied ribbons, all linked by delicate scrolling lines and garlands of husks. Pastel colours were used wherever possible and the graceful, but sometimes anaemic, effect, was in complete contrast to the preceding vigour. This is clearly seen in comparing the looking-glass frame in Fig. 44 with that in Fig. 45.

To match the pale-tinted backgrounds, furniture was made much less substantial in appearance than hitherto. Not only did the designers strive to achieve this effect, but before long the rich red-brown of mahogany was being alleviated by light-coloured borders and inlays, and finally was almost completely banished.

Woods that had been long-established fell into disuse, while others in which interest had been only slight suddenly came into demand. Because of their clear straight markings, which were ideal for use in cross-banding, tulipwood and rosewood were brought from the tropics where they grew; the first-named with reddish lines on a creamy-yellow ground, and the other with black on brown. The wood gaining the greatest popularity was one that finally ousted almost all others for a decade or two: satinwood.

Satinwood has a very distinctive yellow colour with silky markings of a lighter tone, which give it a likeness to the fabric whence it acquired its name. It came from two sources; the East and the West Indies, the latter variety reaching England first and said to have been preferred by cabinet-makers. In the last quarter of the eighteenth century it was employed principally for veneering, with the exception of such parts as the arms and legs of chairs which were cut from logs. Being of a light colour, the wood made an admirable background for marquetry, and it was also suitable for painted decoration. This was fashionable for a time, and much of the work was painted in oil-colours direct on to the wood surface. Alternatively, engravings, hand-decorated in watercolours, were stuck down and varnished within borders of inlay or painting. The fashion for furniture in this style was revived towards the end of Queen Victoria's reign, and the supply of genuine pieces was heavily augmented by reproductions. These, and others closely resembling eighteenth-century examples, can sometimes baffle all but the expert, so painted and inlaid satinwood articles should be examined with particular care to establish their authenticity.

During the second half of the eighteenth century English cabinet-makers attained a mastery of their craft that has never been excelled. There was an extension to the range of articles that were made, while existing types were modified to conform to the demands of an increasingly high standard of living. From the Continent came

36 Mahogany 'Ribband
back' chair after a design
by Thomas Chippendale,
see Fig. 100, page 108.
About 1755.

37 Side-table, the top of
inlaid marble, about 1770.
Width 1·32m.

38 Carved walnut side-table, the frieze with a lion mask and skin and the cabriole legs terminating in lion paw feet. About 1735. Width 1·041m.

39 Carved giltwood side-table with a marble top, about 1740. Width 1·752m.

40 Engraved designs for chairs, stools and curtain pelmets, by Daniel Marot; furniture of this pattern, with local variations, was common to England, France and the Netherlands in about 1700.

influences that affected the design of many pieces, both in external shaping and detailed ornament. Reviving an earlier short-lived fashion, carving was frequently replaced by well-modelled gilt bronze mounts affixed to the corners of tables and chests so that they were not only decorative but protected vulnerable parts from damage. Also originating across the Channel was a liking for multi-purpose furniture: pieces adaptable to more than one function. In this category are Pembroke tables with a bank of concealed drawers and pigeon-holes that rise up from the top when a button is pressed, and tables and chairs ingeniously convertible into library-steps. Later, there were sofa-tables containing small pianofortes, and others instantly transformed for reading, writing or playing various games from chess to backgammon.

The finish of these and other pieces was frequently of the highest quality. The best carving in mahogany had earlier resembled chiselled bronze, and now the detail of doors and drawers was little less perfect. Drawers usually embodied the additional refinement of a cock-beaded edge, and some were given quarter-round mouldings running along the inner bottoms of the sides. The cock-bead, a narrow strip of wood with a rounded edge projecting on the front of a drawer, had been first seen in the 1730's, but the other moulding, which gave added strength, did not appear until about 1800.

The next change in furniture design took place during the early years of the new, nineteenth, century, when the results of a reappraisal of classical art began to be seen. The style is conveniently known as Regency, although the actual duration of that historical event was only from 1811 to 1820, when the Prince of Wales succeeded to the throne as George IV. In modern times the period has been stretched for convenience to cover from 1783 to 1830; the dates in question being those when the Prince attained the age of 21 and the year of his death.

The earlier work of Adam and his followers had constituted a revival of the decorative motifs of ancient Greece and Rome, but this later generation went deeper into the subject. They recreated chairs, tables and other furniture which was, so far as possible, precisely in the shapes used some 1,500 years earlier. Thus, the type of seat in which Roman magistrates heard cases and pronounced judgments, the curule with its curved X-frame, formed the basis for stools and chairs which provided comfort in the drawing-rooms of fashionable homes.

Prominent as a designer was Thomas Hope, son of a

41 State barge with carved gilded ornament, designed by William Kent for Frederick Louis, Prince of Wales, and built in 1731–2.

42 Marble-topped console table in carved giltwood, designed by William Kent for Chiswick House, London, in about 1727. Width 69·8cm.

Dutch banker, a refugee from the French occupation of Holland, who published engravings of the furniture he had had made in the surroundings in which it was displayed. He owned houses in London and at Dorking, Surrey; the plates in his book, *Household Furniture*, referring to the former. Hope's preoccupation with design and the studied arrangements he depicted caused him to be described by a contemporary satirist as 'The man of chairs and tables, the gentleman of sofas'.

The Regency did not limit its explorations of the past to any particular country or period, and its great variety is one reason for its appeal to so many later collectors. When Napoleon invaded Egypt in 1798 he took with him not only an army but a band of artists and archaeologists, whose booty proved more lasting than that of the cavalry, infantry and gunners. Books of engravings of Egyptian treasures were duly published to provide material for designers in France and, after an interval, in England. Crocodiles and sphinxes appeared on cabinets, looking-glass frames and much else, while obelisks and lotus plants were equally fashionable ornamental motifs. The successful exploits of Admiral Lord Nelson inspired a further flood of decorative details, this time of nautical emblems including carving of rope form, dolphins and anchors, which were especially popular following the death of the national hero at Trafalgar in 1805.

Brass handles and escutcheons came into use towards the end of the seventeenth century, and varied in pattern no less than did the articles they adorned. At various times, plain polished wood knobs were employed in place of metal handles, and the keyhole entry was framed by a simple narrow outline, flush with the surface, instead of a shaped plate fitted on the front. In modern times brass has always been preferred, and has invariably been used to replace wood pulls. Traces of the latter are usually clearly visible inside a drawer-front, but such substitution, if reasonably neatly carried out with fittings of correct pattern, should not detract from the appearance or the value of a piece of furniture.

The Regency saw the re-appearance of a style that had first achieved a limited recognition in the mid-eighteenth century. It was known as Gothic and was based on medieval architecture, the various features such as lancets, cusps and crockets being applied to all kinds of articles from bookcases to armchairs. Its most notable adherent was Horace Walpole who, in the 1750s even went so far as to give some of the rooms of his house, Strawberry Hill, Twickenham, vaulted ceilings and other features more often found in churches than in homes. In the Regency a small quantity of furniture was made in the same manner, and the period also saw the birth of A. W. N. Pugin, who became an architect and a great exponent of the Gothic style. Pugin was responsible for much of the detailed ornament in the Houses of Parliament, which were rebuilt following a disastrous fire in 1834, and he also designed some Gothic furniture.

Interest in Chinese objects, which had continued throughout the eighteenth century, was also apparent during the Regency. The Prince himself led the fashion from his Oriental-style Pavilion at Brighton, which he packed with treasures from the Far East as well as with English-made articles inspired by them. Thus, there was truly something for everyone at the time, whatever his or her personal taste. Added to this wide range is the fact

43 Cabinet and chest of drawers, mahogany inlaid with engraved brass and mounted in gilt metal, probably by John Channon, about 1745. Width 1·117m.

44 Overmantel mirror in
a carved giltwood frame of
Rococo design, the picture
dated 1761. Width 1·245m.

45 Oval mirror in a
frame of neo-Classical
design, about 1775. Width
81·3cm.

that so much of the furniture was of a small size readily
usable in modern homes, so it is understandable why
Regency pieces are so eagerly sought that many of them
are priced out of the reach of an average buyer.

While much of the furniture made in the first quarter
of the nineteenth century was veneered with exotic woods
of various kinds, many chairs, and some other pieces,
were of beech. This was decorated in black paint and
gold or in colours, frequently being grained to simulate
rosewood. The latter wood was very popular when used
in conjunction with brass inlay in the manner of the old
Parisian maker, A. C. Boulle. Its employment in England
at the time was doubtless due to the presence of skilled
French craftsmen who had crossed the Channel following
the Revolution in their native land.

By 1825 the simpler, and to many people today the
most attractive, features of Regency furniture were being
supplanted by carving. Well-marked wood was still being
selected for the best pieces, the standard of workmanship remained as high as ever, but a heaviness of
appearance was taking hold. The fronts of sideboards

56

and tables often centred on large-sized bulging ornament, and there was a tendency for mouldings to lose
their earlier grace and subtlety.

Until the reign of William IV furniture had mostly
been finished by hand-rubbing it smooth with various
abrasives, such as brick dust, followed by linseed oil and
beeswax. In due course, after further waxings, the
surface admired by future generations was obtained, but
this was a slow and costly way of achieving such an end.
Along with other innovations from France came the
process known as French polishing: the application by
means of a pad of a type of varnish made from shellac
dissolved in spirit. It was also a laborious process and a
skilled one, but the result was more immediately attractive, giving a surface with much greater brilliance
than had been formerly attainable. Little wonder then,
that French polishing quickly gained acceptance, although
in fact it proved less durable than the old method. Much
antique furniture has from time to time been stripped
of its carefully-tended layers of protective wax to emerge
from the workshop with a hard coating of shellac; a
treatment that is regretted by a discriminating minority
who appreciate a surface literally reflecting the solicitude
of past generations.

A feature seen from about 1820 was the turned straight
chair leg. Slightly prior to this, the curved sabre or
scimitar leg was the rage, and earlier still the pre-1750
cabriole had given way to a tapered straight leg. Then,
from about 1840 the cabriole returned, although this
time it was more slender and resembled the French Louis
XV version. The foregoing are only approximate dates,
for all furniture was made to suit a buyer. While there
were times when most tastes coincided, exceptions
abounded, and there were straight legs to be found on
1750 chairs as well as cabrioles when simple tapering
supports were apparently universal.

The dining-table also changed its form once again so
that it would seat all the company, as had been the
custom in earlier times. The type in use in the last
decades of the eighteenth century was made in two or
more sections fitting together and with extra leaves that
might be inserted, the whole being held together with
brass clips across the joins. Each of the parts was raised
on a turned stem above a base with three curved legs
terminating in carved paw feet or brass caps with castors.
By 1820 the arch of the 'Pillar-table' leg had altered in
shape to include a hump on the knee, and there were

A HARLEQUIN PEMB...

46 Inlaid satinwood
bow-fronted cabinet,
about 1780. Width 81cm.

47 Engraved design for 'A Harlequin
Pembroke Table', published by
Thomas Sheraton, 1792.

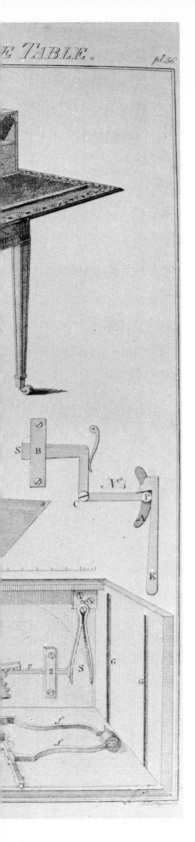

alternative varieties of table that extended on the pantograph principle.

Wealthy buyers had always selected whatever furniture they wanted by choosing it from drawings or printed designs and having it made especially, although the cheaper grades of goods might be bought by them ready-made. From the early eighteenth century, the modern system of shops stocking a range of finished articles spread rapidly. From the 1830s onwards they were supplied by the newly-established concerns which manufactured in bulk to suit the requirements of the rapidly increasing mass of the population. While the owners of great houses continued to have their furnishings supplied on a personal basis, the vast majority was mass-produced for the teeming occupants of the expanding cities and their suburbs all over Britain.

Unquestionably the introduction of steam power played a large part in augmenting the production of furniture. Saws were certainly operated by it and saved time and human labour, but mechanical carving did not come into use, except in isolated instances, until after 1851. Nevertheless, carving and plenty of it was the keynote of furniture in the mid-century. At the Great Exhibition, held in London in 1851, there was displayed a selection of ostentatious pieces from all over the world, each nation vying with the other to show the most extravagant examples of its craftsmanship and catch the eye of as many as possible of the 6,039,195 visitors. The panel of judges who pronounced on the furniture was under the chairmanship of the President of the Austrian Imperial Academy of Fine Arts, and included representatives from Russia, Belgium, Sardinia, Germany and England. Its report is an interesting contemporary comment on the productions of that time or any other:

> It is not necessary that an object be covered with ornament, or be extravagant in form, to obtain the element of beauty; articles of furniture are too often crowded with unnecessary embellishment, which, besides adding to their cost, interferes with their use, purpose, and convenience; the perfection of art manufacture consists in combining, with the greatest possible effect, the useful with the pleasing, and the execution of this can generally be most successfully carried out by adopting the simplest process.

48 Satinwood 'Harlequin Pembroke Table', a variation on the design in Fig. 47.

49 Brass-inlaid rosewood games table, the top inlaid with a chess board and beneath it a removable backgammon board. About 1805. Width 1·213m.

50 Cock-beaded drawer front.

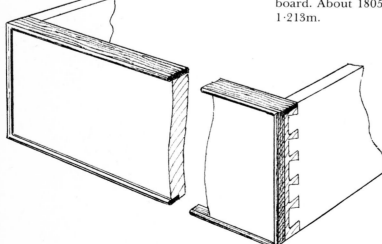

51 Drawer showing dovetails and inside moulding.

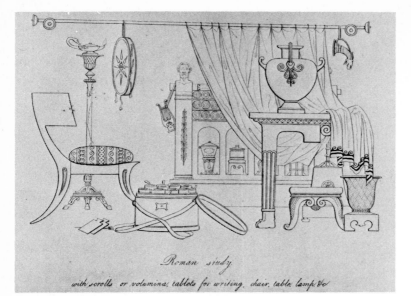

52 'Roman Study, with scrolls or volumina, tablets for writing, chair, table, lamp, &c.', by Thomas Hope.

53 Mahogany armchair, the arm supports carved as winged lions, from a design by Thomas Hope published in 1807.

54 Rosewood two-door cabinet, the frieze inlaid in brass and the side columns with Egyptian heads and feet. About 1815. Width 94cm.

55 Mahogany breakfront bookcase with Gothic-style ornament, about 1830. Width 5·64m.

56 Mahogany chair with
sabre legs and 'rope'-carved back bar,
about 1810.

57 Black japanned
cabinet on stand,
decorated with Chinese
scenes in colours, about
1810.

64

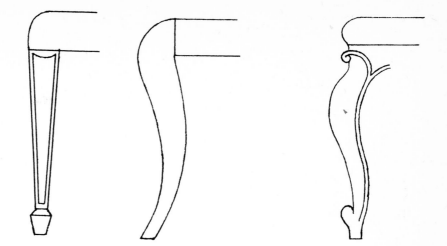

58 Chair legs: (left to right), 1730, 1780, 1810, 1850.

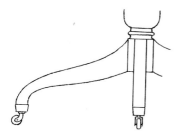

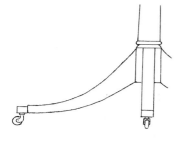

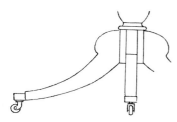

60 Dining-table legs: (top to bottom), 1800, 1810, 1820.

59 Mahogany four-part dining table on pillar supports, about 1800–10. Width 1·422m.

61 Woodcut of a mahogany sideboard shown at the Great Exhibition, 1851, by Gillows of London and Lancaster.

The Cabinet Maker.

Workshops and Showrooms

There is all too little contemporary material from which it is possible to learn what an old cabinet-maker's workshop was like and how it was run. In a small book for young readers, first published in the early 1800's, the craft is explained thus:

> The cabinet-maker is but a superior kind of carpenter; he works neater, is employed on better materials, and his gains, whether considered as a master or journeyman, are probably much greater than those of a common carpenter. The cabinet-maker represented in the plate is one that makes chairs, tables, looking-glass frames, bookcases, &c. His chief tools are saws, axes, planes, chisels, files, gimlets, turn-screws, hammers, and other tools, which are used in common by the carpenter and the cabinet-maker: but those adapted to the latter are much finer than the tools required by the house-carpenter. The workman represented in the plate is in the act of making a looking-glass frame; he is putting some glue on one of the side-pieces, in order to fix it in the hole that is prepared to receive it.

The wood-cut illustration shows bench, tools and glue-pot that can still be paralleled in design in many present-day workshops, and were probably little different a century earlier. The secretaire-bookcase standing on the left is of the usual late eighteenth-century pattern and in the foreground of the picture, perhaps deliberately

62 Woodcut of a cabinet-maker, 1823; the same illustration was first published as a copperplate engraving in 1804.

63 Interior of the Dominy family workshop showing their workbench and tools, removed from East Hampton, Long Island and now reconstructed at Winterthur, Delaware.

drawn out of scale so as not to take up too much space, are an armchair and a bedside cupboard of the same period.

A more vivid impression can be gained from the Dominy workshop, which is now installed in the Henry Francis du Pont Winterthur Museum, Winterthur, Delaware. Although it was used by Americans on American soil, there is no reason to suppose it differed in any material way from hundreds of similar establishments of the same date in England.

The Dominy family is known to have settled in the seventeenth century at East Hampton, Long Island, about 100 miles from New York City. In 1669, Nathaniel Dominy, thought to be of English origin and the first of the line to bear the same forename, was married in the little town. He seems to have been a farmer, while his grandson who died in 1778 was described in documents as a carpenter. The son of this carpenter, Nathaniel

64 The Dominy family workshop, the workbench seen in Fig. 63 is on the left and above it hang templates such as were used in shaping the legs of the finished table in the centre.

Dominy IV, who lived between 1737 and 1812, certainly used the workshop, which is known to have been added by 1760 to the rear of the wood-built house that had been erected earlier. Until 1946 it still contained the tools and equipment, as well as account books and other records, once the property of Nathaniel IV, his son Nathaniel V, and his grandson Felix Dominy. Felix died in 1868, but later generations continued to own and live in the house until its condition deteriorated so much that it had to be demolished.

At the museum in Winterthur the workshop has been painstakingly re-instated to resemble the original as closely as possible. The many tools acquired and used by the three generations of occupants have been sorted to exclude any made after 1850. Of those of the preceding 100 years that remain, fifty-five, including forty-seven planes, bear the date of their manufacture or acquisition. Most of the tools were imported from England, as

American-made supplies were either scarce or non-existent at the time, although in some instances the wood handles and other parts were made by one or other of the Dominys.

In the illustration of the workshop in Fig. 64 there is a row of planes on a shelf over the door at the end of the room. In the foreground is the lathe on the right, while on the left is the big wheel that was its driving force. The lathe was made by one of the family in the third quarter of the eighteenth century, and was used for all kinds of furniture parts: chair and table legs, and so forth. The wheel would have been turned by anyone available when it was required, but the task was probably assigned to a junior while learning his trade.

The Dominys also had a simple pole-lathe for less exacting work, which can be seen at the back on the right. It could be driven by the operator with his foot, thus leaving his hands free to hold chisels. The pole-lathe was worked by means of a treadle, and above it was fixed a long springy pole from the end of which hung a ring of rope. This was wound round the stock of the lathe, so that it returned the treadle to its starting position as soon as foot-pressure on it ceased.

In the centre of the workshop there stands a mahogany tea table on a tripod base, the circular top hinged and with a brass spring-catch to allow it to tip-up when not in use. The stem and top were both turned, probably on the big wheel lathe; the whole was the work of Nathaniel Dominy V in 1796. This particular table is not recorded in his account book as it was made for the use of his family, but for comparable examples he is known to have charged 24s. or 34s. (£1.20 or £1.70).

In its general appearance the table resembles those made in England up to 40 years earlier, but allowance must be made for the fact that East Hampton was a country town in a distant land and fashions changed very slowly so far away from London. For making legs and any other shaped parts of furniture for which there was a recurrent demand, cabinet-makers would keep a stock of templates: flat wooden outline shapes that saved the time of drawing each one individually. Some of the Dominys' templates are seen hanging from the rafters over the bench on the left, and they no doubt gave good service over a considerable period.

An English country workshop would have resembled that of the Dominys in its contents and appearance, but while the former may have been closer to a big city it

65 Chair constructed of ash and elm, probably early 19th century.

70

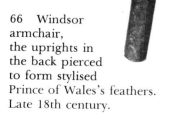

66 Windsor
armchair,
the uprights in
the back pierced
to form stylised
Prince of Wales's feathers.
Late 18th century.

71

would also have been isolated. Roads throughout the British Isles remained somewhere between poor and impassable during most of the eighteenth century, and transport of goods overland became quick and cheap only with the coming of railways. The country cabinet-maker relied for clients on the area where he worked, and he was equally cut-off for supplies of anything other than native timbers. Much of his output comprised simple chairs, tables and chests for cottages and the secondary rooms of houses. Many of the articles, being plain and with no pretentions to be anything but functional, have long ago been discarded. Some examples remain, like the chair in Fig. 65, which is made of elm and ash and has a flat wooden seat. It is almost undatable with its lack of features that can be assigned to a particular period, but was probably made in about 1800.

Almost equally ageless is the Windsor chair, with its stick back and legs which were usually turned but sometimes were cabrioles. In the late eighteenth century some London makers specialised in them and related rustic articles, the chairs being employed in taverns as well as outdoors. Lock[n]. Foulger had a printed label announcing that 'he makes and sells all sorts of Windsor chairs, garden seats, rural settees, &c.', and illustrating some of them. The use of the term 'Windsor chair' has been traced back to the 1720's, but their type of construction goes back in time much farther. A large industry in chair-making centred on High Wycombe, Buckinghamshire, during the nineteenth century, where the surrounding beech woods gave employment to itinerant turners known in the locality as 'bodgers'. Patterns of Windsor chairs changed little over the years, and while there are variations in details only the brief fashion for Gothic produced a noticeable difference. For a while, between about 1750 and 1770, the backs became lancet-shaped, rising to a point in place of the normal curve. Although made principally of beech, the seat of the Windsor was usually of elm, while the central member in the back, known as the splat, was frequently of yew. Yew was used also to form the bow of the back, but as an alternative ash was sometimes employed.

Cabinet-makers who fared better for both materials and clients were those established in provincial cities, seaports or, in the later eighteenth century, in districts served by canals. If a cabinet-maker had the skill and ambition to do better, as in other trades he migrated from the countryside to join those thronging the capital;

67 Miniature mahogany extending dining table, the mechanism patented by S. Hawkins, of a type shown at the 1851 Great Exhibition. Width 22·2cm.

those who were described in 1771 as 'country fools' induced 'to quit their healthy clean fields for a region of dirt, stink and noise'.

Even if a country landowner wanted to patronise a cabinet-maker in his own locality, whether near a town or a small village, it was generally out of the question for him to be supplied with anything except goods of a comparatively ordinary description. They would probably be well-made, but lacking in the refinements to be found in similar articles from London. It was to London that wealthier buyers turned automatically when they furnished their new houses or re-equipped them. In London, there was an ample selection of large and small establishments catering for all tastes and pockets. Most of the shops were grouped in districts that retained a reputation for them over the decades, and sometimes for a century or more.

During much of the eighteenth century the area immediately surrounding St. Paul's Cathedral, known as St. Paul's Churchyard, was the home of many furniture-dealers, but later St. Martin's Lane took its place. There,

68 Miniature settee of mahogany, made by S. Aarons, Spitalfields, London, in about 1845. Length 61cm.

at the sign of The Golden Chair, later no. 60, were the premises of the most esteemed of all English cabinet-makers, Thomas Chippendale. By the 1820s there had been a further migration westwards, following in the wake of new house building, to Bond Street, although at all times the discriminating were catered for by firms with what may be termed unfashionable addresses.

As with other trades, there were two distinct classes of cabinet-makers: masters and journeymen, the former employing the latter. A man could by law become a cabinet-maker only after serving an apprenticeship over a period of seven years, as enacted by the Statute of Artificers in 1563. For, it was stated 'Until a man grow into 23 years, he for the most part, although not always is wild, without judgment and not of sufficient experience to govern himself', but in 1814 this was apparently no longer thought to apply and the Elizabethan statute was repealed in so far as it made apprenticeship a condition of employment. A master made a charge for taking an apprentice and this ranged, according to the status of the former, from about £20 upwards. In return, the youngster had to be taught the trade, was usually paid a wage and given bed, board and medical attention.

69   Design for a 'Grecian couch' published by J. C. Loudon in 1833.

All this, and sometimes more, was set out in the indenture between the parties, which was a document liable to a charge for duty.

It has been suggested that an apprentice would make a small-scale piece of furniture to prove his prowess, but there is no evidence that this was a general practice. Many antique miniature specimens survive, and while some of them may have been the work of apprentices, there can be little doubt that others were demonstration models. The mahogany dining-table in Fig. 67 has an extension mechanism operated by winding with a key. On a part of the simple mechanism is engraved: 'S. Hawkins Patent 140'. In the catalogue of the Great Exhibition of 1851 is the entry:

> Samuel Hawkins 54 Bishopsgate Street Without
> Patentee and Manufacturer
> Model set of expanding tables to show the adaptation of the patentee's patent screw movement by which one person can open and close any size dining-table.

A woodcut illustration shows the mechanism, and on another page of the same catalogue is the information that a full-size table with Hawkins's action was also on show. It was made and exhibited by William Smee & Son, of Finsbury Pavement, a well-known firm which was in business during most of Queen Victoria's reign. From this it would appear that the table illustrated is either the actual example shown in the Crystal Palace, or was one of a number placed in shops to obtain orders.

Another miniature is shown in Fig. 68. It is inscribed in ink under the framework of the seat 'J. Aarons Maker

Samuel Burton

UPHOLDER & CABINET-MAKER,

in St. Mary Ax near Leadenhall Street,

London.

Makes & Sells all Sorts of Cabinet & Upholstry Goods,
in the genteelest & newest Fashion, in Silk and Worsted
Damask Furniture, Mohair, Morine, and Cotton Ditto,
with all Sorts of Cheque, Harrateen, &c. Feather Beds, Hair
& Flock Matrasses, Counterpanes, Cotton Quilts, Blankets, &c.
Chests of Drawers, Desk & Book Cases, Wardrobes,
Dining Tables, Card Ditto, and Commode Dressing
Tables, Chairs, Looking Glasses, &c.
Turkey, Wilton & other Carpets, for Home use or Exportation.
Variety of Paper Hangings.

GOODS APPRAISED and FUNERALS FURNISH'D.

70   Trade card of Samuel Burton, active between about 1768 and 1793.

15 Freeman Street Tenter Ground Spitalfields'. The little mahogany settee is of similar pattern to one illustrated in a book published in 1833, J. C. Loudon's *Encyclopaedia of Cottage, Farm and Villa Architecture*. A heaviness in the legs and the different shape of the curve of the back point to a date in the region of 1845. It may well have served the same purpose as the dining-table, in advertising the wares of its maker. Earlier specimens than the foregoing are recorded, but nothing is known of their original purpose, which may have been simply to please lovers of the miniature.

The journeymen were not invariably a contented body of workers, as for instance in 1761 when they went on strike for higher wages. They were followed a year or so later by the house-carpenters, of whom it was sympathetically remarked: 'The poor fellows, whose all their labour is, see their masters advance their prices every day, and think it reasonable to touch their share'. As

71 Trade card of Ann Buck, widow of Henry Buck who died in about 1750.

72 Walnut joint-stool made in the area of Boston, Massachusetts, in about 1700. Height 58·4cm.

73 English-made oak joint-stool, about 1650. Height 49cm.

alliances of work-people were illegal, these disaffections received very little publicity at the time, although Parliament issued an Order that magistrates should prosecute the owners of public-houses where the strikers resorted.

Strictly speaking, the term 'cabinet-maker' would apply to a maker of good-quality furniture, but in practice it extended to cover those who retailed such goods and were not necessarily concerned in their making. Likewise, there is ambiguity in the descriptive word 'upholsterer', which applied normally to a man who made curtains and stuffed chairs and other seat furniture. From printed references to the two, it seems that the terms were largely interchangeable in the past. A writer in 1811 noted:

> . . . in almost all places the business of the cabinet-maker is united to that of the upholsterer; and the furniture collected in one of their warehouses, is worth from ten to thirty thousand pounds.

Some of the bigger London cabinet-makers were suppliers of everything connected with furnishing, and their premises embraced workshops for many trades

74 Oak cabinet ornamented with mouldings, carving and applied turnings, the front bearing the initials T S B for Thomas and Sarah Buffington, and dated 1676. Perhaps made by James Symonds, of Salem, Massachusetts. Height 44·5cm.

that were otherwise specialist crafts. In the case of large orders for country mansions it is known, however, that there was a considerable amount of sub-contracting. No single workshop or group of them was of a size sufficient to cope with a really extensive contract and it was only practicable to share it.

Chippendale was not alone in his day in supplying his clients with fine furniture as well as curtains, cornices, carpets, cushions and feather-beds, and also sending men into the provinces to do paper-hanging and similar jobs. In addition, he and many others in the later eighteenth century carried on the earlier tradition of cabinet-makers in furnishing funerals. Following a death, many cabinet-makers also provided black hangings for a room in which a body lay. The trade card of Samuel Burton, whose premises were in Leadenhall Street, in the City, depicts a hearse and horses, all plumed, followed by two carriages, proceeding to a church seen in the distance.

Seddon's, of Aldersgate Street, also in the City, had extensive workshops and showrooms which were viewed by a German visitor in 1786. Frau Sophie von La Roche fortunately wrote down her impressions, and they form a vivid catalogue of what she saw. On September 16th she noted an invitation to see a friend at Windsor, but before going there she went to Seddon's, of which she recorded:

> He employs four hundred apprentices on any work connected with the making of household furniture—joiners, carvers, gilders, mirror-workers, upholsterers, girdlers—who mould the bronze into graceful patterns—and locksmiths. All these are housed in a building with six wings. In the basement mirrors are cast and cut. Some other departments contain nothing but chairs, sofas and stools of every description, some quite simple, others exquisitely carved and made of all varieties of wood, and one large room is full up with all the finished articles in this line, while others are occupied by writing-tables, cupboards, chests of drawers, charmingly fashioned desks, chests, both large and small, work- and toilet-tables in all manner of wood and patterns, from the simplest and cheapest to the most elegant and expensive.
>
> Charming dressing-tables are also to be seen, with vase-shaped mirrors, occupying very little space, and yet containing all that is necessary to the toilet of any reasonable person. Close-stools, too, made like a tiny chest of drawers, with a couple of drawers, decorative for any room. Numerous articles made of straw-coloured service wood and charmingly finished with all the cabinet-maker's skill. Chintz, silk and wool materials for curtains and bed-covers; hangings in every possible material; carpets and stair-carpets to order; in short, anything one might desire to furnish a house; and all the workmen besides and a great many seamstresses; their own saw-house, too, where as many blocks of fine foreign wood lie piled, as firs and oaks are seen at our saw-mills.

It may be queried whether glass would have been cast there, in the basement. The furnaces required for melting the material would not have been accommodated in such a place, especially as the entire building had been burnt to the ground in 1783. However, it is likely that Seddon had facilities to cut and bevel plates of glass brought from an outside source. In mentioning service-wood, which is fruit-wood used sometimes for small turned goods, Sophie (or her translator from German

75 Mahogany
serpentine-fronted card
table, the frieze fitted with
a drawer and carved with
gadrooning at the edge,
made by Thomas Affleck,
Philadelphia. About 1770.
Width 91·5cm.

76 Mahogany lowboy, an
American version of earlier
English dressing tables (as
in Fig. 23, page 31) and
probably by a Maryland
maker in about 1770.
Width 89cm.

77 Mahogany chair in the style of Hepplewhite, made by Jens Brøttrup, Copenhagen. A label on it gives his address as Store Fiolstraede No. 186, where he was in business between 1784 and 1802.

78 Design for a shield-back chair, from Hepplewhite's *The Cabinet-Maker and Upholsterer's Guide, 1788*.

into English) is mistaken; the wood would most probably have been satinwood. Furthermore girdlers had no connexion with mounts for furniture, and the term bronze-casters would be more appropriate.

Men like Chippendale and Seddon, who were in control of a series of workshops and showrooms and catered for the full range of furnishings, would not have worked at the bench once they had become established in business. Their role was to attend clients in the showrooms or their homes, estimate costs and, if a buyer lacked his own or his architect's ideas, suggest suitable ones. Sketches would be submitted, and orders awaited. When all was delivered and approved, the cabinet-maker normally endured the torment inflicted on all traders in the past: he awaited payment. Many of the surviving letters of Thomas Chippendale refer to his anxieties in this direction, and it was without doubt this unfortunate custom that led so many cabinet-makers to the bankruptcy court in the eighteenth century.

As well as the large-scale all-round cabinet-makers, there were lesser men who were solely furniture retailers. There is no way now of distinguishing between them and those who were actual working cabinet-makers, as both retailers and makers described themselves similarly. This is not to say that anyone was telling an untruth by calling himself 'cabinet-maker' when in strict modern parlance he was nothing of the sort, but the English language and its usage have changed over the last two hundred years. In the interval many fine distinctions have vanished while others have emerged.

It is uncertain how many of the hundreds of retailers in the past included second-hand goods in their stocks. Ann Buck, whose card bears the head of a stern-looking Queen Anne at the top, stated clearly that she 'buys and sells . . . all sorts of household furniture, old and new' and does not, for once, call herself a 'maker'. In the days before shops specifically sold 'antiques', it is likely that other cabinet-makers catered for buyers wanting the old-fashioned or unable to afford the new. There have always been retailers who congregated in a particular street or district and specialised in the second-hand. Thus, in 1768 Lady Mary Coke was busy finding furniture for her recently-acquired home in Kensington, and near Moor-fields, in the City, she visited 'a place called Broker's Row, where I bought several things; my Coach was almost filled'.

Not until the early 1830s is there a clear indication of the existence in London of a good number of equivalents to modern 'antique' shops. A writer in 1833 mentioned the firm of Nixon & Sons, of Great Portland Street, who specialised in the Louis XIV style; one that was commented on as being 'unsuitable for persons in moderate circumstances'. The same source also listed Wilkinson of Oxford Street, Hanson of John Street, and Kensett of Mortimer Street, all of whom stocked a selection of Elizabethan furniture and carvings, from the latter of which 'a judicious compiler of exteriors might clothe skeleton frames, so as to produce objects of curiosity and interest, at a very trifling expense'.

London-based working cabinet-makers of the eighteenth century were conveniently placed for exporting their products by way of the Port of London. From there goods were sent to Spain and Portugal, the countries of

79   Mahogany chair in the Hepplewhite style, London made, about 1790

80 Mark of Jean-Henri
Riesener, the most famous
of French cabinet-makers.
He was born in 1734 and
died at some time after
1800, having become a
member of the Guild of
Cabinetmakers in 1768.

81 Gilt gesso table with
the crowned cypher of
George I at the front,
signed by James Moore,
whose surname is carved
on it. About 1715.

*By gracious permission of H.M. the
Queen*

Scandinavia, Russia, and far afield to the East and West
Indies and North America. In 1700 various types of furniture, ranging from cabinets to nests of trunks, were
sent abroad through the Port of London and assessed
at a total of about £33,000, plus a further £2,000 for
articles sent from other ports. The figure was £38,000
a century later, and although in 1800 Napoleon was at
war with Britain the French still imported furniture from
England but only to the value of £33.

Most of our present-day knowledge of this traffic has
been found as the result of research into Customs
records, there being very little mention in the press of
that time. The few exceptions include a paragraph in a
newspaper in 1731 reporting a fire in Clerkenwell, by
which the cabinet-maker, Giles Grendey, had furniture
destroyed to the value of £1,000 which was 'pack'd for
Exportation against the Morning'. The intended destina-
tion of the goods was not mentioned, but in the present
century some of Grendey's furniture has been discovered in countries as far apart as Spain and Norway.
The firm of Ince & Mayhew is known to have sent furniture to Denmark, and some examples remain there.

This trading was not entirely in one direction. Both
Thomas Chippendale and Ince & Mayhew issued their
books of designs in English and French, and the latter
makers informed clients that 'they have an assortment
of French furniture consign'd from Paris, for immediate
sale, very much under the original cost, which may be
seen at their warehouse, Broad Street, Soho'. Chippendale is known to have imported French chairs, and there

was an inquiry in Parliament in 1772 following a complaint by some London master and journeymen cabinet-makers. They alleged they were losing business because of the activities of two foreign ambassadors who were importing French furniture duty free by pretending it was for their personal use. The furniture was being offered for sale in the showrooms of a number of prominent cabinet-makers, and following the receipt of positive evidence of the state of affairs Customs officers promptly seized the contraband goods.

By the end of the eighteenth century, good cabinet-making had become established in some provincial towns. Among them, Lancaster, some 50 miles to the north of Liverpool, was noted in 1776 as being 'famous in having some very ingenious cabinet-makers settled here, who fabricate most excellent and neat goods at remarkably cheap rates, which they export to London and the plantations'. Robert Gillow began to work there in 1730–40 and by 1765 had opened a branch in Oxford Street, London, which bore the name into the present century. Leeds has been shown to have been the centre of several flourishing workshops in the nineteenth century, while Edinburgh was far enough from the capital to have supported a full array of cabinet-makers and upholsterers of its own from an earlier date. They were fewer in number than those in the far south but their quality of workmanship was high and in many cases their designs were distinctive. In spite of this availability of good class local work many owners of Scottish mansions filled their principal rooms with furniture from London.

Furniture closely following English designs was also made in countries abroad, especially those where there was a high proportion of settlers from the British Isles. In North America, the followers in the footsteps of the Pilgrim Fathers must have taken with them whatever they could find space for in their small ships, and this would have included a quantity of furniture. On the whole, such imports would have been slight, and reliance was placed on what they could make for themselves once they had built their homes. These pieces would have differed only slightly from their prototypes, the use of particular woods, such as red oak, which was native to America, often providing the clearest evidence of their source.

The joint-stool in Fig. 72 is a copy of an English oak example of about 1650, but there are important differences between them. That in Fig. 73 is of English origin, but the other was made in the area of Boston, Massachusetts, in about 1700, and is of American walnut. The small cabinet in Fig. 74 is initialled and dated TSB 1676, and was probably made in the town of Salem, in the same state. It is constructed of oak, cedar and maple, whereas the English equivalent would have been almost certainly entirely of oak and would be datable to about the mid-seventeenth century.

Later American-made pieces often continued to resemble London originals. The mahogany card-table in Fig. 75 was the work of the Philadelphia cabinet-maker, Thomas Affleck, while the Maryland lowboy in Fig. 76, although of a distinctive American type, has basic English features.

Furniture of late eighteenth-century English style was made in Copenhagen where a Dane, Jens Brøttrup, after a period of training in London, had premises in Store Fiolstraede. He was trading there between 1784 and 1802, and advertised himself as 'English cabinet maker and chair maker'. One of Brøttrup's mahogany chairs in the Hepplewhite style is shown in Fig. 77, and in Figs 78 and 79 are the original design and an English-made version of it.

Finally, there was the German-born Abraham Röntgen, who also trained in London, where it is known he was resident between 1731 and 1738. He later set out to emigrate to Carolina as a missionary, but was ship-wrecked on the way and returned to Neuweid, near Frankfurt, in his native land. There he made good quality furniture in the English manner, much of it inlaid with ornament in engraved ivory and mother-of-pearl and with fine lines of brass. His son, David, took over the workshop at Neuweid in 1761, specialising in the first instance in pieces with elaborate marquetry ornament and then in desks and other articles with complex mechanical features. He became a member of the Parisian Guild of Cabinet-makers, opened branch establishments in Berlin, Brussels and St. Petersburg and was in receipt of commissions from important buyers in many European countries. His furniture is of high quality, but in appearance is unquestionably of Continental origin. Despite this fact, and although he is not known to have visited England at any time, he termed himself *'Englische Kabinettmacher'*. That he did so, is a sterling tribute to the eminence of eighteenth-century English craftsmen.

82 Printed label of John Coxed, about 1700.

83 Printed label of G. Coxed and T. Woster, the former probably a relative of John Coxed.

Cabinet-makers 1

The makers of old English furniture only occasionally rendered it possible for later generations to recognise their productions. In view of this, the task of identification has not usually been attempted and pieces have been put into categories such as 'Chippendale', 'Sheraton' and 'Hepplewhite', although up to the present time nothing whatsoever has been identified as the work of the two latter. However, in recent years, long-overdue research into the lives of the men and their output has been undertaken and published, largely stimulated by the Furniture History Society, and it may not be so long now before our knowledge of English furniture approaches that of French furniture.

The identification of the makers of French furniture has been in progress since 1882. In that year, at a large exhibition held in Paris it was noticed that many pieces of fine furniture on display were stamped, usually in out-of-the-way places with names and other marks, and some examples had semi-concealed painted or branded insignia, letters and numbers. The discovery of these long-overlooked signs set scholars to work, and as a result a great deal of information has gradually been assembled.

Each stamped mark was identified as the name of the maker responsible for that piece and, where it appeared, a further mark denoted that it had been inspected and had reached the required standard of craftsmanship. It was also discovered that the numerals and insignia tallied with entries in the carefully-kept archives of the palaces of Louis XIV, Louis XV and Louis XVI. In many instances it became possible to learn not only who had made an article, but the exact dates on which the work was ordered and completed, what it cost and precisely in which room of a named mansion it had been duly placed. Details of the lives and careers of some hundreds of makers were slowly brought to light, and today the names of Riesener and many of his fellow workers are known internationally. It may be added that this has had its drawbacks, for no sooner were the facts known than the value of signed pieces rose and, predictably, the forging of marks began.

The French cabinet-makers stamped their productions not with an eye to future historians and collectors, but because of the strict regulations of their powerful guild. In 1741 there took place a re-drafting of the rules, and thenceforward every member was compelled to possess a metal stamp bearing his name, or sometimes only his initials, with which he must mark every piece of furniture he made or repaired. The number of members was limited to under a thousand at any one time, and entry was not only expensive as regards fees but each potential member had to submit a sample of his work for approval before being accepted into the ranks.

Four times a year every member's premises were visited and the finished productions inspected by a small panel of guild members. Provided the goods reached the required standards of workmanship they were then further stamped with the guild mark: the conjoined initials J M E, for *jurande* or *juré menuisiers-ébénistes*, which is briefly translatable as 'jury of joiners and cabinet-makers'. Exceptions to this rule were those persons who supplied the Crown, and others who were established in certain districts declared free of the guild's jurisdiction. In the case of the latter, buyers were unprotected, and the quality of workmanship could not always be relied upon, although prices might be lower because the makers did not have to pay any guild fees. Where it operated, the system was equivalent to the hall-marking of silver, and it offered a similar safeguard to the purchaser (Fig. 80).

In England no such control existed after the guilds or companies weakened their hold, which began to take place in the fifteenth century. Standards were kept high largely through competition, and a man who knew his trade thoroughly usually prospered. Royal patronage

84 Bureau-cabinet veneered with burr mulberry-wood and inlaid with lines of pewter, made by John Coxed. About 1700. Width 96·5cm.

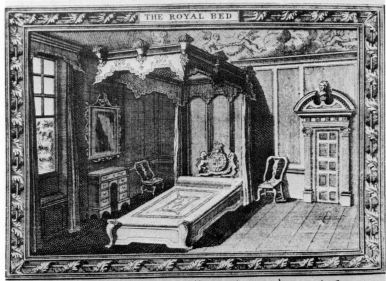

85 Trade card of Nash, Hall and Whitehorne, active between about 1720 and 1750.

was sought, as an appointment was a valuable seal of approval and was cherished once it had been gained. Tradesmen served the households of the monarch as well as members of his or her family, and others were appointed to the Great Wardrobe: an office concerned with the provision of furnishings of all kinds for the Court, Ambassadors and numerous other dignitaries. In the later seventeenth century the Wardrobe had at its command an annual sum of £25,000, so that its powers of patronage were extensive.

The names of many of the late seventeenth- and early eighteenth-century makers are known from records of their charges, although the majority of the actual furniture has gone despite its having existed in quantity. It has been pointed out that 'in the course of centuries furniture, at least of certain types, has proved more perishable than pictures'. Considering the comparatively harder wear-and-tear suffered by tables and chairs and other articles this is understandable.

With the passage of time, such bills and records as were kept, and in big establishments it was the practice to retain everything, were often forgotten and lay con-

GILES GRENDEY,
St John's Square, Clerkenwell,
LONDON,
MAKES and Seils all Sorts of CABINET GOODS, Chairs Tables, Glaſſes, &c

86 Printed label of Giles Grendey (1693–1780).

cealed in a muniment room when the articles to which they referred were sold. There are some instances, notably a few pieces of furniture in Royal ownership, where the articles remain together with contemporary information as full as that noted in France. From these it has sometimes been possible to identify pieces that resemble them in appearance and age.

Such identifications, which are based mainly on a similarity in design, are not invariably reliable. A feature of any kind was quickly copied, and after a very short lapse of time it would become difficult or impossible to distinguish the prototype from its imitations. More certain identification of a maker is practicable when a piece of furniture is labelled. From the later seventeenth century a proportion of cabinet-makers and others used pieces of printed paper for the purpose, but there would appear to have been an unwritten rule, as in France, that a cabinet-maker did not advertise his name on goods supplied to Royalty. There are a few exceptions to this, one of them being a gilt-framed tall looking-glass at Hampton Court, which bears the surname of its maker, John Gumley, on a small cross-piece of wood in the border. Another is a gilt gesso side table now at Buckingham Palace, but which was originally housed across the park in Kensington Palace. On the front of the table is the cypher of George I framed by the Garter motto beneath a crown, and above the crown is the surname of the maker, John Moore (Fig. 81). Some candlestands and a table at Hampton Court also bear Moore's name, which is neatly carved in the same way amidst the ornamentation.

John Gumley is one of the first cabinet-makers whose name appears in print elsewhere than at the top of an invoice or at the foot of an advertisement, for he received mentions from Sir Richard Steele, a respected prominent author and playwright of the day. Gumley not only sold 'all sorts of cabinet work', but soon after 1700 he was operating a looking-glass manufactory. In 1714 he took premises in the Strand, of which Steele wrote praising the display of mirrors; recommending them as being the best obtainable and to be purchased for 'a trifle'. Soon after Steele wrote his words of praise a young man paid a visit to Gumley's and noted frankly in his diary:

> There is indeed a noble collection of looking-glass, the finest I believe in Europe. I could not as I passed there help observing myself, particularly my manner of walking, and that pleased me very well, for I thought I did it with a very genteel air.

Gumley supplied some mirrors to the Duke of Devonshire, at Chatsworth, Derbyshire, where they remain, and on one of them is scratched his name and the date 1703. From 1714 John Gumley was in partnership with James Moore who, as noted above, signed some tables and candlestands. Some of Moore's work is authenticated by surviving records, and he is known to have been employed by Sarah, Duchess of Marlborough, during the building of Blenheim. The Duchess referred to him as her 'oracle; of very good sense . . . .'.

At the dates when Gumley and Moore were flourishing, a number of makers who wished to advertise themselves were occasionally attaching to their goods labels printed with their names and addresses. Some of the labels are of simple pattern, small size and briefly worded, while others are elaborate and often depict and describe the types of goods retailed. How, and under what circumstances, they were used cannot be gauged, as many have doubtless been removed in the past and the proportion of pieces originally bearing the labels is indeterminable. Fortunately, quite a number have been preserved and recorded, and a study of them has greatly helped to increase present-day knowledge of one-time cabinet-makers and their productions.

The plainer type of label is typified by that of John Coxed, of The Swan, St. Paul's Churchyard, which bears at its foot in small type: Cluer, in Bow Churchyard, Printer of all sorts of Advertisements (Fig. 82). John Coxed took over the premises in about 1700 from a Mr. Hayes, an upholsterer, and at the same address in about 1715, G. Coxed, perhaps a son of the foregoing,

87 Card table on cabriole legs with lions' paw feet, in the manner of Giles Grendey. About 1740.

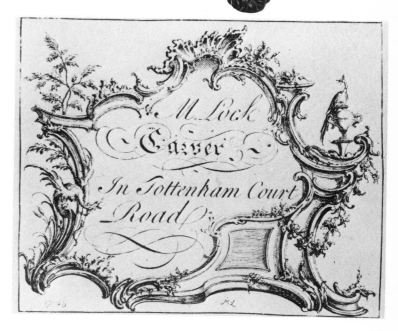

88 Trade card of the carver Matthias Lock.

89 Trade card of Henry
Jouret, frame-maker and
print-seller, engraved and
doubtless also designed
by Matthias Lock.

acquired Thomas Woster as a partner. Coxed and Woster
used similar labels from the same printer (Fig. 83), but
the wording concludes with the information that they
sold their goods 'at reasonable Rates', and the woodcut
has been changed. The frame is of a different pattern
with leaves at the base, while the swan is no longer
placidly swimming but stands on land angrily with its
beak open, tongue protruding and wings upraised.

The labels of Coxed and Coxed & Woster have been
discovered on several pieces of furniture with features in
common. Most of them are in the form of a bureau-
cabinet with mirror doors, veneered with panels of
mulberry-wood within kingwood cross-banding and
inlaid narrow lines of pewter (Fig. 84). Mulberry is a
wood with strong light and dark markings, and un-
labelled pieces of comparable age and appearance are
attributable to the same makers, who would seem to
have made a speciality of this distinctive combination
of veneers and metal inlay.

As has been remarked earlier, it is seldom possible to
be absolutely certain if a man calling himself a cabinet-

90 Giltwood side-table,
the frieze with a mask of
Hercules draped with the
skin of the Nemean lion,
which he strangled as one
of his twelve Labours.
Resembling a drawing by
Matthias Lock of about
1740. Width about 1·80m.

94

maker was an actual producer of goods or a retailer of other men's work. In isolated instances there is little or no doubt, and an advertisement in the pages of the *London Journal*, in January 1720, is clearly inserted by a retailer, for no mention is made of a maker. The advertiser was a Mr. Normand Cany, of whom nothing else is recorded, and he informed readers that the fine bed earlier exhibited at Somerset House, in the Strand, was now to be seen at Exeter Exchange, in the same thoroughfare. The notice was concerned to describe the hangings, which were the most valuable part, and read as follows:

> This bed is wrought with the most beautiful feathers of divers colours, woven into a stuff: so that the curtains are as light, and as manageable, as if they were of damask. ... Each curtain has a purple border of a foot broad, branched with flowers clouded with scarlet. ... The corners of the bedstead, and the four vases, which rise on the tester, are adorned with festoons and flowers in relief. In short, this is such a curious piece of workmanship, as cannot be paralelled by any hand whatsoever. This, with several other curious and beautiful pieces of the same kind as the said bed, are to be seen ... there are likewise several fine pictures, by the best hands, to be sold; all which may be seen at any hour of the day, each person paying two shillings and six pence.

Reverting to labels, doubt creeps in again. The label in Fig. 85 is in contrast to the simpler examples already

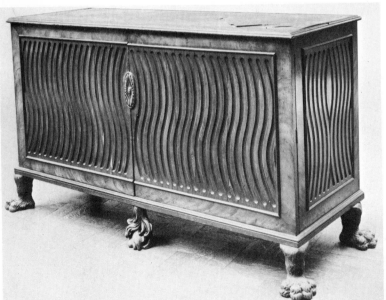

91 *Top left* Cabinet
on stand, veneered with
amboyna-wood, inlaid with
brass and mounted in gilt
metal, probably by John
Channon. About 1745.

92 Bureau-cabinet
decorated with Chinese
scenes on a black ground,
made by John Belchier in
about 1730.

93 'Sarcophagus-like
Cabinet' of mahogany
supplied by Robert Tuson
in 1772, the central lion's
tail was added in 1775.
Width 1·117m.

94 Label of Philip Bell in
a drawer of the chest in
Plate 5 (page 101),
about 1770.

Philip Bell

at the WHITE SWAN againſt

the South Gate in S.ᵗ Pauls Church Yard

London.

Makes & sells all sorts of y.ᵉ finest Cabinet Goods,

all sorts of Looking Glasses, Coach Glasses, & Chairs

of all sorts, at Reaſonable Rates.

NB. Old Glaſses new Wo̶r̶k̶ up Fashionable

95 Later label of Philip Bell, engraved by Matthew Darly who supplied some of the copperplates for Chippendale's *Director* and other books of Rococo designs.

illustrated, but in spite of the wording 'make and sell' there is no guarantee that the firm did the first. Thomas Nash was in business at least from 1722, and his premises, *The Royal Bed* were on Holborn Bridge, which crossed the Fleet and Holborn streams and was situated just north of the present junction of Farringdon Road and Holborn. The engraved picture shows a bedroom of about 1730, the half-tester bedstead, with its two supports for the tester in place of the four of a four-poster, has the Royal arms as a headboard, there is a kneehole dressing table in the room, two chairs with cabriole legs, and a looking-glass in a carved frame. Many a bedroom in a large house must have resembled it at about that date, although probably its occupant would gladly have exchanged the cupids painted on the ceiling for a rug or two on the floor.

Another straightforward and simple printed label is that used by Giles Grendey (Fig. 86): noted earlier (page 84) as having had some of his finished goods destroyed by fire in 1731 when they were packed for export. Grendey is known to have been born in 1693, was a member of the Joiners' Company, of which he became Master in 1766, and died at the age of 87 in 1780. A few bills for furniture he supplied have been preserved but not the articles to which they refer, while, of more importance, some labelled pieces are known. A large red lacquered suite comprising a day-bed, six armchairs and twenty single chairs was discovered in Spain in 1935; one of the armchairs, which is now in the Metropolitan Museum, New York, bears Grendey's label. Similar pieces are in

98

the Victoria and Albert Museum, London and at Temple Newsam House, Leeds (the latter in Plate 1, page 17).

Labelled articles include a mahogany cupboard and a lacquered cabinet, both of which have door-panels of similarly shaped outline, and some pieces with carved friezes of a particular pattern (Fig. 87). The unorthodox spelling of names and words prior to the nineteenth century often hinders research. On one of his bills Grendey's name is spelt 'Greenday, chair maker', in a 1753 directory entry he appears as 'Grindey', and on the occasion of the marriage of his daughter he is described as 'timber-merchant'. As this last event took place in 1755 he may by then have given up making furniture, for it is presumed he had his own workshop, in favour of dealing in the material from which it is made.

96 Trade card of William Henshaw, active between about 1755 and 1770, the 'Ribband back chair' in the centre bears a close resemblance to those of Chippendale (see Figs 36 and 100).

It would seem that the more important the cabinet-maker the less likely it was that he used labels on his productions. Such was the case with William Hallet, who had a highly successful career, and newspaper references to his name invariably couple it with the adjective 'eminent'. Some of his work is to be seen at Holkham, Norfolk, and more is in a number of other great houses, although not all that is enumerated in his accounts has been identified. Only one item bears anything like a 'label': his name written in pencil, on a part of the interior of its base. The scrawled inscription, 'William Hallet 1763 Long Acre', was found by chance some years ago when damage necessitated taking apart the lower section of a mahogany cabinet. Whether Hallet himself wrote the words is unknown, and the reason for their appearance in such an obscure place is equally a mystery.

As early as the end of the seventeenth century lived a man who gained lasting fame as a wood carver. Grinling Gibbons was born in Rotterdam and came to England in about 1670. There, in a cottage at Deptford, outside London, he was found by John Evelyn, who recorded in his diary how he discovered the man carving in wood a Crucifixion scene. Evelyn was very impressed by his skill, and introduced him to Court, where he was eventually appointed Master Carver. Much of his work has been preserved, although more examples than he himself executed have been credited to him at one time or another.

The introduction of mahogany in the 1730s and its suitability for carved ornament, led to a greater demand for carvers and to the establishment of a number of men specialising in the art. Among them was Matthias Lock, who first came to public notice as the creator of some Rococo ornaments, tables and wall-mirrors, designs for which were published in the form of thin booklets of engravings between 1740 and 1746. They were in the Rococo style, which was then new to England, and Lock was in the vanguard of its early exponents. He designed his own trade card with his name set within a Rococo frame, and also designed and engraved one in the same style for a frame-maker and printseller, named Henry Jouret (Figs 88 and 89).

A large number of original drawings by Matthias Lock are in the Victoria & Albert Museum, others are in New York, in the Metropolitan Museum, and he issued a few further engravings up to 1769, after which no more is heard of him. A large looking-glass and side-table in the Victoria & Albert Museum not only correspond to

Plate 5 Mahogany serpentine-fronted chest of drawers made by Philip Bell, about 1770. Width 1·105m.

Plate 6 Mahogany secretaire-bookcase with carved boxwood ornament, made by Henry Kettle, about 1780. Width 1·067m.

Plate 7 Rosewood bookcase, one of a set of four supplied by Banting, France and Co., in 1829. Complete with marble slabs the four cost a total of £632 3s. 6d. Width 2·21m.

Plate 8a Mahogany library table with gilt metal mounts, by J. M'Lane and Son, about 1810. Diameter of top, 1·067m.

97 Queen Charlotte's jewel-cabinet, of mahogany veneered with padouk and other woods inlaid with ivory, made by William Vile and John Cobb in 1761.

By gracious permission of H.M. the Queen

sketches there, but scribbled against the drawings are rough notes about the hours taken over the work and the names of those who performed it, including that of Lock himself as carver.

A gilt side-table conforming in many details to one of Matthias Lock's drawings is illustrated in Fig. 90. The head on the frieze is that of Hercules, and draped about it and beside it is the skin of the allegedly invulnerable lion of Nemea, which he strangled. Other tables of closely similar pattern are known, and it is not improbable that Lock designed and carved them all.

Experts had for a long time been puzzled as to the origins of a small number of very unusual pieces of furniture, extremely well made from carefully selected

wood, inlaid with engraved brass and mounted in gilt
bronze. Then it was remembered that in a room at
Powderham Castle, Devon, stood a pair of bookcases in
the same style, each bearing a small plate inscribed 'J.
CHANNON 1740'. Research resulted in the information
that there had been an Otho Channon, a chair-maker
in Exeter, whose son John set up in business in St. Martin's Lane, London in about 1737. He was living in the
same house until 1783, but very little more is yet known
about him. The recorded pieces of furniture are all of
unusual pattern, the quality of the workmanship being
enhanced by the exotic woods from which they are made.
Rosewood and amboyna, both of which were costly at
that time, played their part, and the use of metal mounts
was not common then in England (Fig. 91, and page 46).
In general appearance the work so far attributed to

Channon has a noticeably foreign air, and it has been remarked of the Powderham bookcases that they 'would not look out of place in an early eighteenth-century South German Baroque interior'; words that are applicable no less to the other pieces. Doubtless more facts about this maker and his career will eventually come to light; having been forgotten for two centuries he is now beginning to receive due recognition as an outstanding craftsman.

John Belchier lived slightly earlier than John Channon, and his furniture, although of good quality, does not differ from that made by many of his contemporaries. He used a printed bill-head with the wording: 'All sorts of Cabbinet Work, Chairs, Glasses, Sconces, and Coach-Glasses, made and sold at reasonable rates by John Belchier, at ye Sun on the south side of St. Paul's, near Doctors Commons', and at the top is a benign looking sun within a circle of rays. In addition he placed on some of his work a small label stating simply that he had made the article and appended his name and address.

Belchier is mentioned in some letters written in 1735 by a lady living in Buckinghamshire who ordered from him an overmantel mirror, 'a glasse in a gold frame three foot eleven inches and an half long by twenty four inches, the middle glasse to be thirty one inches long', for which she was charged £3 16s. The mirror was of a type common at that date, comprising two narrow pieces of glass flanking the principal large plate, all in a gilt wood frame. Also fashionable then was lacquered furniture, and some examples are known bearing Belchier's label (Fig. 92). Information about him is otherwise slight, apart from the fact that he is recorded as having died in 1753 'aged near seventy years'.

While most buyers purchased their requirements in a complete state from a cabinet-maker, it was not unknown for some to have their own timber made up. One instance of this is revealed in the accounts of Charles Rogers, a man whose career was spent in the Customs and who lived in Laurence Pountney Lane in the City. He lived between 1711 and 1784, died a bachelor, and a portion of his collection of works of art of all varieties, together with some papers, was bequeathed by a descendant of his sister's husband to the City of Plymouth. They are to be seen there in the Museum and Art Gallery.

On 22nd July 1757 Rogers noted the purchase of 'a Log of yellow Brazil Wood' for £1 3s. 6d., and in

November of the same year he gave £2 19s. 0d. for 'Vaneers of wood'. No mention is made of what particular woods supplied the veneers, but 'yellow Brazil Wood' would have been a South American timber mostly valued for providing a yellow dye but also occasionally employed by cabinet-makers. It is likely that working at the Custom House gave Rogers the chance of occasionally buying imported woods.

The bookcase in Plate 3 (page 35) is one of a matching pair at Plymouth, and there is a third of much larger size. All of them match in having the door-frames veneered with amboyna, and it seems highly probable that they are referred to in this entry in the Accounts:

> 26 Oct 1757 Paid Mr Wood two Amboina Cabinets
> & other Work   70.00.00.

Charles Rogers paid for other articles, including a cabinet, a table and 28 picture-frames, all of which were veneered with the same wood, but the work was executed by another man, Robert Tuson.

Tuson supplied also what he aptly described as a 'Sarcophagus-like Cabinet' in December 1772 (Fig. 93), for which, with some unspecified items he was paid a total of £17 15s. 0d. The width of the article must have caused it to sag slightly in the centre and make the doors stick, so there is a further entry referring to the same piece of furniture:

> 17 Jan 1775 Paid Mr R. Tuson for a Lion's tail of Mohogony carved for the Sarcophagus 17s.

So far no other mention of either Thomas Wood or Robert Tuson has been discovered.

Thomas Woster was mentioned above as being in partnership with G. Coxed in premises in St. Paul's Churchyard. He died in 1736 and the shop, *The Swan*, now *The White Swan* was then taken by another cabinet-maker, Henry Bell, whose label was more decorative than that of his predecessors. The wording on it concludes with 'N.B. Old glasses new worked and made up fashionable', which meant that he would re-frame and, if necessary also re-silver, old mirrors. This was a service that Bell was not alone in offering to perform, as plates of mirror-glass if at all large were costly and re-silvering and re-framing comparatively cheap. Not only did the client obtain his glass returned in a condition as good as new but it would be framed in the very latest style.

In about the mid-century, Henry Bell was succeeded by his wife, Elizabeth, who carried on the business under her own name. She had the copper plate used for printing the label altered accordingly, but otherwise it was left unchanged. It was, incidentally, not at all unusual for a wife widowed during Georgian times to continue a business that had been her husband's. Perhaps the best-known instance, is that of Hester Bateman, whose husband died in 1760 when she was only 51, and the lady-silversmith took over the business for the ensuing 30 years. It is improbable that either Mrs. Bell or Mrs. Bateman worked at the bench themselves, their roles being limited to supervision of suitable managers and craftsmen.

In about 1760, Henry Bell's original *White Swan* label, was again changed to become that of Elizabeth Bell and Son. It was unaltered except for the addition of '& Son', and the same occurred in about 1765 when the name changed to Philip Bell (Fig. 94). It is most probable that Philip was a son of Henry and Elizabeth and the use of the same copper plate, with minor changes, for printing the label of all three would confirm this supposition.

However, Philip Bell discarded the much-used label,

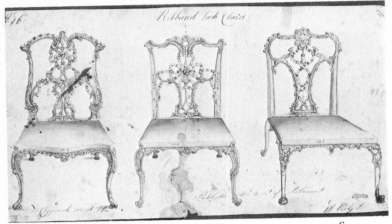

100 'Ribband back Chairs', drawing by Thomas Chippendale which was engraved for the 1754 edition of his *Director*.

perhaps because the plate had become too worn for successful printing, and had it completely re-designed. As can be seen in Fig. 95 it was much more up-to-date than the other, with a Rococo frame for the wording flanked by a cabinet and an armchair in the Chinese and French styles respectively. At the top appear two hatchments to underline the legend 'N.B. Funerals perform'd', which replaces the earlier offer to re-silver and re-frame looking-glasses. Philip Bell's earlier label is affixed inside a drawer in the chest in Plate 5 (page 101).

After 1773 houses and shops, hitherto identified by signs, gradually began to bear numbers. As a result *The White Swan*, became No. 18, St. Paul's Churchyard, and was duly occupied by yet another member of the same trade, Henry Kettle. Kettle, it appears, then moved to No. 23 and took as partner William Henshaw. A namesake of the latter, possibly his father or even the same man, was also 'on the South side of St. Paul's Church Yard', as is clear from the very fine label he used at that address (Fig. 96). The china cabinet depicted in the upper part of the elaborate Rococo framing has in front of it a 'Riband-back' chair, which is remarkably close in pattern to one designed by Thomas Chippendale (see left-hand chair in Fig. 100, above). The label dates from about 1760 not long after Chippendale had published his engraving.

Henry Kettle remained at No. 23 until 1796, so that following those who had occupied No. 18 he was a direct successor to the Mr. Hayes, upholsterer, who had come in 1696. It is an extreme example of the continuity that was not uncommon in the past, when a shop would descend from father to son or, at any rate, remain for a long period stocking the same type of goods.

In 1750 the most eminent cabinet-making firm was

that of William Vile and John Cobb, whose workshop and showroom were on the corner of St. Martin's Lane and Long Acre. None of their labels, if they used any, have been found, but examples of their workmanship are known from documents. William Vile supplied the Crown, and some of his productions remain in Buckingham Palace; he supplied them when that mansion had been bought by George III in 1762 and was thenceforward known as the Queen's House. The cabinet which he made for containing the jewels given by the King to the Queen and worn at the Coronation in 1761, was invoiced by the partners as follows:

> For a very handsome Jewel Cabinet made of many different kinds of wood on a Mohog^y Frame very richly Carved all the Front, Ends & Top Inlaid with Ivory in Compartments & neatly Ingraved the Top to lift up & two drawers under the doors all lined with fine Black Velvet with fine Locks & the Brass Work Gilt £138. 10s.

The veneers comprise padouk, amboyna, rosewood and tulipwood, and the top of the cabinet is inlaid in

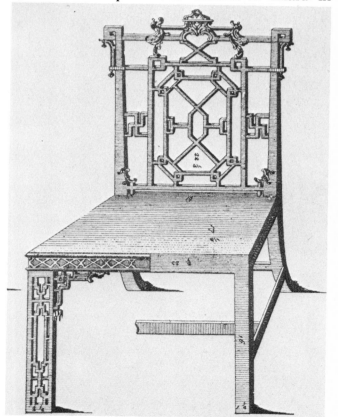

101 Engraving for a 'Chinese Chair' from Chippendale's *Director*; the back incorporates Rococo scrolls among Chinese frets and tiny bells.

102 Mahogany secretaire-cabinet supplied by Chippendale, Haig and Co., in 1774 at a cost of £3 8s. Width 1·245m.

engraved ivory with the arms of Queen Charlotte (Fig. 97).

Other, less sumptuous, pieces known to have been supplied by Vile are characterised by the high quality of their finish, and the use of carved ornament which was often in the form of swags of flowers. Another favoured feature is a central circular or oval panel in the front of cabinets, chests and other articles (Fig. 98).

William Vile was in business with John Cobb, and some of their bills were rendered jointly. Shortly before the death of Vile in 1767 and the disappearance of his name from the Royal accounts, it is noticeable that he was not replaced by Cobb. A little is known about the latter from a description of him printed in 1828, where it was said of him by a fellow-craftsman:

> Cobb was perhaps one of the proudest men in England; and always appeared in full dress of the most superb and costly kind, in which state he would strut through his workshops giving orders to his men.

A marquetry commode at Corsham, near Bath, was supplied to the house in 1772 and Cobb's bill for it is preserved. A few very similar pieces are known, one of which is illustrated in Fig. 99, and are attributed to the same maker. Cobb died in 1778, some six years after his name had been mentioned in connexion with the smuggling of furniture from France and goods had been seized from his showroom. Whether this event hastened his end or a foreknowledge of it kept the Crown from patronising him, is not known.

103 Giltwood settee, part of a suite probably supplied by Thomas Chippendale in about 1770. Width 2·54m.

Cabinet-makers 2

The name of Thomas Chippendale is linked in most minds with the very best in English furniture, and he is deservedly famous as a designer and maker. For many people almost all old mahogany pieces are 'Chippendale', yet the truth is that only a very small proportion of surviving examples can be attributed to him with certainty. Much more is known about his work than about his life, and even the little recorded about the latter is frequently erroneous.

In the registers of the parish church of Otley, Yorkshire, is the entry of the baptism on 5th June 1718 of Thomas, son of John 'Chippindale', a joiner. Thomas is said to have started his career by working for his father, and it is alleged that his genius was recognised by the Lascelles family, of nearby Harewood House, whose interest and influence enabled him to become established in London. Alternatively, he is stated to have been employed by Sir Rowland Wynn, who was building his mansion, Nostell Priory, near Wakefield and some 30 miles from Otley, from 1733 onwards. His connexion with either or both of these important Yorkshire patrons is problematical, although in later life he certainly numbered both families among his clients.

The next positive evidence confirms that he had reached London. For on 19th May 1748, at the age of 30, he was married to Catherine Redshaw, who was apparently a Londoner and bore her husband eleven children before dying in 1772. From then onwards, a

104 Rosewood sofa table with lyre ends, made by Thomas Chippendale the Younger in about 1800. Width 1·63m.

little more detail is available concerning his life. At Christmas 1749 he is known to have been living just off Long Acre, and four years later moved southwards to an address in a lane next to Northumberland House. This Jacobean mansion stood in the Strand at Charing Cross until 1874, when it was demolished to make way for Northumberland Avenue.

Then, late in 1753 Chippendale took a 60-year lease of premises in St. Martin's Lane, and in the following April appeared his book of furniture designs, *The Gentleman and Cabinet-Maker's Director*. The large-sized volume contained 161 engraved plates, with designs for a variety of pieces from chairs to bookcases, and in styles owing their inspiration to France, China, and the creators of medieval Gothic buildings.

Such a complete pattern-book was a new departure; nothing comparable had ever been available for English makers. In the early pages it included a List of Subscribers: those who previously had agreed to purchase copies once it was published, and these include a good number of cabinet-makers. Thus, it became possible for any one of them, in whatever part of the country he had his workshops, to produce goods in a style equal to that of London. To make sure that he did not lose his own clients to other craftsmen, Chippendale concluded his Preface thus:

> I am confident I can convince all Noblemen, Gentlemen, or others, who will honour me with their Commands, that every Design in the Book can be improved, both as to Beauty and Enrichment, in the Execution of it, by Their Most Obedient Servant, Thomas Chippendale.

Most of the numerous engravings in the *Director* are signed 'T. Chippendale inv^t et del', implying that he devised and drew the original design, while the man who executed the engraving added his name in the opposite corner. It has been argued that the cabinet-maker was perhaps only responsible for a proportion of the work, and that the real originators of the more ornamental designs were Matthias Lock (see page 100), and a man with whom Lock had collaborated in publishing some

105 Wood-seated hall chair designed by William Ince and engraved in Ince and Mayhew's *Universal System of Household Furniture*.

106 Stamped mark of Gillows, Lancaster, about 1810.

107 Mahogany wine table with reeded legs, made by Gillows in about 1810. Diameter 1·728m. After dinner, a table of this type would be placed in front of a fire and gentlemen gathered around it to take their port.

early Rococo engravings, Henry Copland. There is no proof that this occurred, but it is an interesting theory that may possibly one day be found to have a basis in fact. In the meantime, there is nothing to shake Chippendale's claim to authorship of his own drawings.

A number of his designs are in the Victoria & Albert Museum, London, and the Metropolitan Museum, New York. Most of the former were purchased in 1862 and 1863 from the grandson of Matthias Lock, and many of Lock's drawings are intermingled with those of Thomas Chippendale. Likewise, the New York collection, which comprises two albums, contains a number of designs attributed to Lock along with many of Chippendale's; these last being mostly for the 1754 *Director*. In addition to these drawings, a few others recently came on the market (Fig. 100).

Soon after the publication of his book, there appeared a brief paragraph in the press:

> 5th April 1755. A Fire broke out at the workshop of Mr Chippendale, a cabinet maker near St. Martin's Lane, which consumed the same, wherein were the chests of 22 workmen.

From the fact that no fewer than 22 craftsmen lost their tool-chests, it would seem that their master had quickly got himself established on a large scale. How he achieved it so soon is among the many unanswered queries connected with his career.

Possibly unsold copies of the *Director* were victims of the conflagration, for a further edition was issued later in 1755. It is called 'second edition' on the title-page, but differs only in minor details from that of 1754. In August 1759 advertisements in the press stated that the following October would see the publication in weekly parts of another edition, but no copies of it have so far come to light. The third edition finally appeared in 1762, and had a total of 200 plates comprising 95 of those used in 1754, plus 105 fresh ones that took some advantage of changes in style which had taken place in the interim period. On the whole, however, the entire 1762 *Director* remains as true to the Rococo as the first edition of eight years before.

The various engravings depict pieces in a selection of styles: Rococo, (often titled 'French'), Chinese and Gothic. In many cases two or more styles are combined; as appeared for example in a clearly Gothic chair back adorned with little Rococo leaves and scrolls.

Possibly the use of Chinese motifs is most characteristic of Chippendale, and some of his more extreme designs are in this manner (Fig. 101).

Like other eminent cabinet-makers, Chippendale did not use printed labels on his productions, and his work can only be authenticated by surviving documents. His furniture remains, fortunately, in a few of the English mansions for which it was originally supplied, in addition to Harewood House and Nostell Priory mentioned above. A number of his commissions came from Scotland, where some of his pieces stand in the houses to which they journeyed 200 years ago.

Probably for financial reasons Chippendale acquired James Rannie as a partner in 1754, and on the latter's death 12 years later Chippendale traded on his own for a few years. In 1771, Rannie's clerk, Thomas Haig, was taken into partnership, but he was solely concerned with running the office and he played no part in designing and cabinet-making.

In the five-year period between the two partnerships, Chippendale was furnishing Nostell Priory, and his invoices covering the years 1766 to 1771 still survive. They are enlightening for the description of the great variety of goods and services he provided, and in showing that little or nothing was too small to receive attention.

Over the five years the accounts show that he supplied not only a lady's mahogany secretaire-bookcase 'made of very fine wood' for £25, but on 18th February 1767 he sent in a four-post bedstead for the cook's room at 30s. and made a charge of £2 12s. 0d. for 'cleaning furniture, putting up beds and window curtains, fixing a bookcase and sundry jobs'. He supplied and laid carpet (Wilton at 5s. 6d. a yard) and down pillows (8s. each), made curtains, remade mattresses, made leather covers to protect the best furniture when it was not in use, charged one shilling for laying the drawing room carpet, and made for 18s. 'a mahogany house for a monkey'.

Correspondence accompanying the bills shows that all the worries to be expected in equipping a large house were present. Sir Rowland accuses Chippendale of neglect in fulfilling his orders and says he will place his custom elsewhere and concludes in unpunctuated exasperation: 'your behaviour to me is not to be bore & shall take care to acquaint those gentlemen that I have recommended you to & desire that they will oblige me in employing some other person'. In the end everything was delivered, but the cabinet-maker's trials were not at an end, for he had continual difficulty in getting his accounts settled. He pointed out to his client that some of the money had been owed for five years, and that unless it was sent soon 'I shall be utterly ruined'. In fact, he was not beggared, and it must be assumed that all the money was finally paid. It is fair to point out that the delay over money was not entirely one-sided, as Chippendale had to be reminded to submit his bills; he was not only remiss in keeping to delivery dates for goods, but on one occasion took seven months to render an account.

Both in design and execution Chippendale's work is recognised as masterly, so that undoubted examples coming on the open market realise outstandingly high prices. On the other hand, his more everyday pieces also have an unobtrusive distinction about them, even if this is not immediately discernible. The cabinet in Fig. 102 is a good example of his simpler pieces; having a central secretaire drawer that pulls out to form a writing space, and cupboards above and below. When supplied to a Scottish house in 1774 it was invoiced as follows:

> A large mahogany Chiffonier Table off very fine wood with a drawer with Ink and Sand Bottles and a Slider covered with Cloath . . £3. 8. 0.

The few mansions retaining Thomas Chippendale's bills as well as his furniture are exceptional, but there are some where there are bills and nothing else remaining. Thus, at Saltram, Devon, account books record two payments to Chippendale in 1771 and 1772 of a total sum of £170, the second of them being for £50 'on

108   Mahogany writing table, the flat end supports with turned uprights and the curved feet terminating in brass cap castors, made by Gillows. About 1815. Width 96·5cm.

109 Sketch of a 'spindle end' table supplied by Gillows in 1818.

account'. No detailed invoices survive and it is possible only to guess what he may have supplied of the furnishings still in the house. Because it resembles a suite supplied by Chippendale to Harewood House which is fully authenticated, a giltwood suite at Saltram has been thought to be most probably from his workshop (Fig. 103).

The gilt armchair in Plate 2 (page 18) was supplied by Thomas Chippendale to Sir Lawrence Dundas for his house in Arlington Street, London. It was made to the design of Robert Adam, who made a charge of £5 for his drawing. The armchair was one of a set of eight with four matching sofas, and the original bill for them, dated 9th July 1765, totalled £410 4s. This included the provision of leather and cloth cases for the suite when it was not in use, but Sir Lawrence provided his own silk damask for the upholstery.

Thomas Chippendale died in 1779, following a second marriage two years before, and his business was continued by his eldest son, who bore the same name. Thomas Chippendale junior remained in partnership with Thomas Haig until the latter retired in 1796. One of their most important commissions was the furnishing of Stourhead, Wiltshire, where much of their work remains in the mansion (Fig. 104). Supplied just after the turn of the century, the furniture is in the prevailing style, and maintains the high standard of workmanship associated with the St. Martin's Lane establishment in former days.

The second half of the eighteenth century produced a

Plate 9 Brass-inlaid rosewood chess table, made by Banting, France and Co., 1829. At the time it cost £14. Width 83·8cm.

number of cabinet-makers whose work distinguished them from the remainder, and who are also remembered for having published furniture patterns. William Ince and John Mayhew, both of whom are known to have been apprenticed to good craftsmen, set up in business together in 1759 with premises in Broad Street, now Broadwick Street. Later their address was just round the corner in Marshall Street. They were obviously enter-prising, because from July 1759 they issued a series of designs in weekly parts at 1s. each, publishing them in book form about three years later.

The volume was entitled *The Universal System of House-hold Furniture*, and while the designs it contains often reflect those of Chippendale they only rarely equal them (Fig. 105). An innovation was that the title-page, introduc-tion and captions to the illustrations were all printed in French as well as English. Among the surprisingly few pieces of furniture positively identified as having been made by the firm is a mahogany bookcase of about 1760. It is in the Museum of Decorative Arts, Copenhagen, and the label on it reads:

> Mayhew and Ince most respectfully announce that they have an Assortment of French Furniture, con-sign'd from Paris, for immediate Sale, very much under the original Cost, which may be seen at their Warehouse. Broad Street, Soho.

Although George Hepplewhite is also remembered principally by a book of designs, unlike Ince and May-hew none of his work has been identified and not even a bill remains. He is known to have had a cabinet-making business in Redcross Street, in the City, and to have died in 1786, although where and when he was born as well as other details of his life are completely lacking. In 1788 a book, *The Cabinet-Maker and Upholsterer's Guide*, with 128 engraved plates, was compiled 'from drawings by A. Hepplewhite and Co. Cabinet-Makers' and published in London. There is no indication as to who actually executed the original drawings, and for a long time it was assumed that they had been made and bequeathed by George Hepplewhite to his widow, Alice, who duly had them engraved. At any rate, they have given their name to the style of furniture fashionable for a time from 1788. Two further editions of the book were published, of which the third of 1794, contained some revised chair designs. These show the newly-favoured square backs, while the remainder of the volume was unaltered.

Plate 10 Mahogany occasional table, the top composed of marble found in the Palace of the Caesars, Rome, in 1821 (see page 130). Width 74cm.

Most commonly dubbed 'Hepplewhite' are mahogany chairs with shield-shaped backs and square tapering legs (see page 82). Occasionally the backs incorporate a carved motif in the form of the Prince of Wales's feathers, and one such design in the 1788 edition is commented upon in the introduction as having 'been executed with good effect for His Royal Highness the Prince of Wales'. Nonetheless, Hepplewhite's name is not to be found in the Royal accounts, and as the wording quoted does not state categorically that Hepplewhite himself was the maker, the chair was quite possibly made to the design and supplied by someone else.

The Gillow family, as has been mentioned earlier, had workshops in Lancaster from about 1730 and later opened a London showroom. The first of them, Robert Gillow, was succeeded by his sons, Richard and Robert, and between them they were connected with the firm until about 1820. However, the business was later continued with their name included, and by great good fortune most of the records have survived. They go back to the 1740's and include not only copies of letters, but rough drawings, with measurements and other details, of goods supplied to their clients. The 180 volumes in which all these records were contained were sold in 1966 and about to set sail for the United States, when a last-minute rescue was effected to keep them in the land to which, it must be agreed, they belong.

Apart from those instances where furniture supplied by the firm remains in the houses for which it was supplied and is authenticated by bills, Gillows put their name to much of their output from the 1790's onwards. They did not employ the usual printed label, but followed the well-established French method and punched the words GILLOWS LANCASTER in an unobtrusive place. Frequently this was on the upper edge of the door of a dwarf cabinet, or on the top edge of a drawer in a chest (Fig. 106). In modern times these stamped marks have sometimes been removed; as the firm was still in business until the mid-twentieth-century some antique dealers considered that their clients might confuse the modern firm with its predecessors, and to eliminate doubt they would scrape away any trace of the words.

Furniture made by Gillows was invariably well-finished and of carefully selected timber, but it often lacks the refined design of London work. This is to be expected where a workshop was situated so far from the capital, but letters show that concern was felt about it and on an occasion in 1760 a request was sent to London for the latest of Chippendale's designs.

Typical Gillow pieces of the early nineteenth century are shown in Figs 107 and 108. The table is a version of one supplied on 8th November 1818 to Ferguson & Co., of which there is a sketch with details of cost in the Gillow papers (Figs 109 and 110). The present example differs principally in having drawers in the frieze, and would therefore have cost a little more to make than the £5 15s. 4½d. of the other. The firm of Ferguson & Co., were correctly Ferguson, Whitesides & Co., upholsterers, of 176–7 Oxford Street, London, who had taken over the former Gillow premises and were continuing the business under their own name.

When Sophie von La Roche visited Seddon's premises in 1786 (page 79), George Seddon was 59 and had been established about thirty years. In 1768 he suffered a severe loss, as was reported in a newspaper at the time:

> Thursday, 14th June. A dreadful fire burnt down London House, formerly the residence of the bishops of London, in Aldersgate-street, now occupied by Mr Seddon, one of the most eminent cabinet-makers in London. The damage is computed at £20,000.

110 Details of the cost of the table in Fig. 109.

110 Details of the cost of the table in Fig. 109.

Another fire occurred in 1783, when it was said that as many as fifty houses were destroyed and the total damage came to £100,000. Another report of the same event confined the destruction to thirty houses, and concluded with a brief graphic description of the scene:

> At daybreak several families were sitting round what few effects they had saved in Smithfield, some half dressed, and others without clothes, wrapped in carpets and blankets. Several fellows were taken into custody, for purloining the property of the unfortunate sufferers. Fortunately no lives were lost.

On each occasion the business recovered, so that in 1785 a son, George Seddon, was taken into partnership. Later, another son, Thomas, joined the firm, and between 1790 and 1800 they were styled Seddon, Sons and Shackleton, with a son-in-law, George Shackleton as a partner.

In recent years attempts have been made to identify the type of furniture made by the Seddons, but although they must have had a large output little is known about it. Some high quality satinwood pieces have been attributed to them (Fig. 111); possibly because of Sophie von

La Roche's reference to their use of the wood, but also for the reason that they were an eminent firm during the time that satinwood was the height of fashion. The small china- or book-case in Plate 4 (page 36) might have been made by them on account of its excellent workmanship and good design. The way in which the glass is managed in the upper part of the door, lacking uprights so that it runs the full width, is so out of the ordinary that it points to a maker with both skill and originality.

At some date after 1821, when George IV was on the throne, there was a further change in name, and Messrs Morel and Seddon are known to have been the suppliers of furniture to Windsor Castle amounting in cost to more than £180,000. They traded from 16, Lower Grosvenor Street, Mayfair, until 1832, and carried on in various styles from different addresses until as late as 1868.

In the early decades of the nineteenth century, the Seddons occasionally stamped their name on their productions in the form T and G Seddon. They very occasionally screwed on a small brass plaque engraved with their name, and sometimes used a printed label. On the whole, Seddons do not appear to have troubled about advertising themselves and their productions in this way. Like other important concerns, the business flourished sufficiently without their having to use such devices.

Thomas Sheraton, whose surname may be said to be a household word, not only did not label furniture but as far as is known did not make any. Details of his life are not plentiful, but it is known that he was born in 1751 in Durham, at Stockton-on-Tees, and spent his early years as a cabinet-maker. By the early 1790's he was living in Davies Street, London, then in Wardour Street, and finally at Broad Street, Golden Square (now Broadwick Street), where he died in 1806. His Wardour Street card (Fig. 112) makes it clear that he 'Teaches Perspective, Architecture and Ornaments, makes Designs for Cabinet-makers, and sells all kinds of Drawing Books, &c.'. Clearly, he had what might be described as a studio, and not a furniture workshop.

His first publication was *The Cabinet-Maker and Upholsterer's Drawing-Book*, which came out first in parts and in 1793 in book form. In addition to a lengthy section devoted to Geometry and Perspective, the compilation contains designs that are, in the author's words, 'intended to exhibit the present taste of furniture, and at the same time, to give the workman some assistance in the manufacturing part of it'. He does not claim origin-

111 Inlaid satinwood cabinet raised on short tapered square legs, in the manner of Seddons. About 1780. Width 91·5cm.

ality for the pieces he describes and illustrates, and it is not clear what he contributed from his own inventiveness and what he copied from the work of others. The articles he shows have a distinction that must owe much to his own taste and power of selection, so that what is called the 'Sheraton style' is recognisable. Much use is made of inlaid and painted ornament, and the frequent employment of satinwood lends a feminine elegance to most of the designs (Fig. 113).

In 1803 was published *The Cabinet Dictionary*, in which Thomas Sheraton included not only explanations of terms and processes, but entries on irrelevant subjects such as botany. The 88 plates in the book depict furniture that has the gracefulness of 1793 replaced by an incorporation of classical motifs perhaps more suited to stone than wood (Fig. 114). Finally, he issued a single volume of a projected lengthy work, which is a general encyclopaedia with plates of furniture designs that have nothing whatever to do with the text. It is, perhaps, little wonder that an acquaintance described him as:

> . . . a scholar, writes well, and, in my opinion, draws masterly—is an author, bookseller, stationer and teacher . . . I believe his abilities and resources are his ruin in this respect—by attempting to do everything he does nothing.

Although the majority of Royal tradesmen seem not to have put their names to whatever furniture they supplied, there were exceptions to this and among them was John Gee. He had premises in Wardour Street in the first decades of the nineteenth century, and enjoyed the privilege of being 'Turner and Chair-maker to His Majesty', George III. He marked some of his productions by stamping them with his initials, and occasionally with his surname in full (Fig. 115). In so doing he was following a long-standing custom, for from the late seventeenth century it was not unusual for a chair-maker to do this. Richard Price, who supplied chairs and stools to Charles II stamped on them his initials, and in some instances his contemporaries and followers used a heated branding iron for the purpose (see Fig. 31, page 41).

Caution is required with names and initials on furniture because it cannot be taken for granted that they are invariably those of the maker. Owners occasionally marked their possessions in this way, sometimes with the name of the particular mansion to which the piece belonged, and it is not unknown for craftsmen to mark

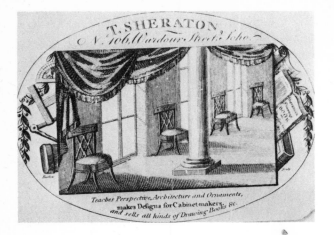

112 Thomas Sheraton's
card, about 1795.

113 Designs for
chair-backs, published by
Thomas Sheraton in 1793.

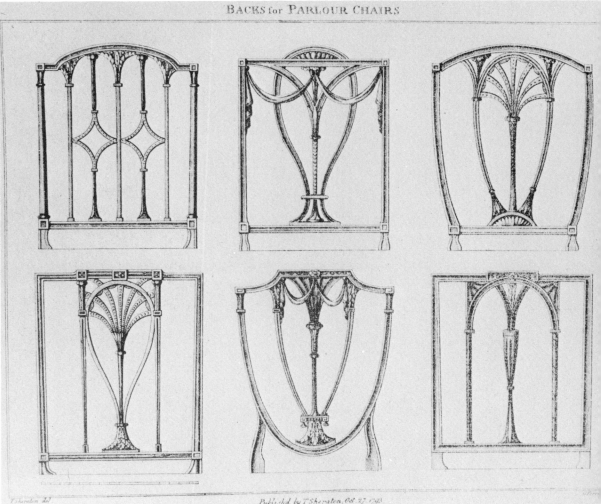

BACKS for PARLOUR CHAIRS

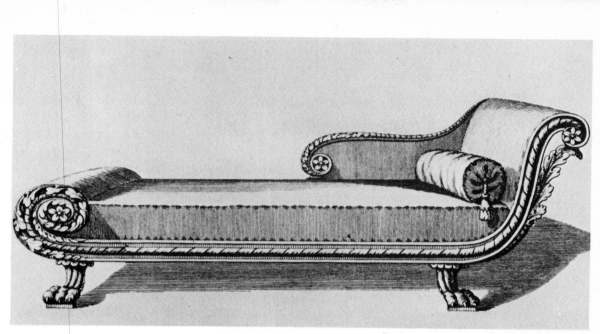

114 'A Grecian Squab';
an engraving dated 1802
and published in
Sheraton's *Cabinet
Dictionary* in the following
year.

115 Painted beechwood
armchair, the frame
stamped with initials J G,
for John Gee, 'Chairmaker
to His Majesty'
(George III). About 1810.

similarly pieces that passed through their hands for repair or sale. Thus the man who stamped some late Georgian furniture with the legend T WILLSON 68 GREAT QUEEN STREET LONDON has been traced trading from that address as 'Thomas Willson, upholsterer' between about 1860 and 1885.

Even when a printed label gives a name, address and other details it is not always easy to place a maker with exactitude. An instance of this is one or more cabinet-makers who between the years 1774 and 1825 bore a surname spelt M'Clean, McLean, M'Lean, M'Lane and Macklane. A printed label of the 1770's reads 'J$^{no.}$ Macklane, Cabinet, Chair Maker and Upholder in little Newport Street, near Leicester Square', and under the same address a list of those who cast votes in the 1774 Westminster election records 'J$^{no.}$ M'Clean, cabinet maker'. In 1803 Sheraton, in his *Dictionary*, recommended 'McLean and Son, Upper Terrace, Tottenham Court Road, and 34 Marylebone Street, Piccadilly', and then stated that work tables are made 'in the neatest manner' by Mr McLean 'in Mary-le-bone street, near Tottenham Court Road'. A further printed label reads: 'John McLean and Son, 58, Upper Mary-le-bone-street, The end of Howland-street, Portland-place', while an 1825 directory gives 'M'Lean William, Upholder 58 Marybone st'.

Not only were the names given in several forms, but the addresses were equally confused. Upper Marybone or Upper Marylebone Street was quite a distance from Marybone or Marylebone Street, and there were at least two streets with the last name, so it is difficult to determine precisely where the firm had its premises.

The games table in Fig. 116 is of distinctive appearance and is one of several known examples which, with a single exception lack an identifying mark as regards their maker. This one bears the printed label of M'Lane & Son, so it is not unreasonable to assume that they all came from the same workshop. The table in question is a well-known one, having been illustrated from time to time in magazines and books since 1926, yet the label, which is placed unobtrusively on the side of a vertical division under the removable top, was completely overlooked for nearly forty years. While it undoubtedly adds to the interest of the piece of furniture to know the name of its maker, the table is unquestionably a fine example of its type and period and the few other undoubted M'Lane productions are of comparable excellence in design and finish.

116 Table partly gilt and painted to resemble bronze, made by J. M'Lane and Son, about 1800. Width 83·8cm. The section of the top marked for chess is reversible and has a leather-covered surface on the other side.

Sometimes a piece of furniture that is neither labelled nor stamped can be dated within close limits from other evidence, such as an inscription. The occasional table in Plate 10 (page 120) is made of rosewood, with a shaped platform base, carved stem and rectangular top; the latter inset in the centre with a chequer-pattern in white and coloured marbles. A drawer in the top has pasted in it a piece of paper on which is written in fading ink:

> The Marbles set in this Table were picked up in the Ruins of the Palace of the Caesars at Rome in January 1821, by John Shawe Manley.

By this, the table can be dated to within a few years after 1821, the returned traveller having had his pieces of marble cut and polished and neatly incorporated in a table of the then fashionable pattern.

A further instance of furniture and bills remaining largely intact in the mansion for which the former was supplied, occurs at Ickworth, Suffolk. The house was built by the 4th Earl of Bristol, Bishop of Derry, who spent most of the years of his life travelling on the Continent and left behind him a trail of hostelries named Hotel Bristol. In 1792, when 62 years old, he visited his family estate near Bury St. Edmunds, and decided to build a mansion there. He died in 1803, before his grandiose plan had reached completion and it was left to his successor, his younger son, the 5th Earl, to eventually make the place habitable.

The furnishing was carried out in 1829 by a firm prominent at the time, Banting, France and Co., 'Upholsterers to His Majesty', George IV. Their showrooms were situated in Pall Mall, and they had workshops nearby in James Street, now known as Orange Street, Haymarket. The majority of pieces supplied by the firm were in the most fashionable wood of the day, rosewood, and their charges, where comparisons are possible, were higher than those of Chippendale's day. In the Library were placed four tall bookcases (Plate 7, page 102), invoiced as follows:

4 large rosewood bookcases	£480. 0. 0.
4 marble slabs for ditto	96. 10. 0.
4 holland covers for ditto	7. 0. 0.
Packing, carriage and mens time	
fix^g Bookcases	48. 13. 6.

The total is £632 3s. 6d. or just over £150 apiece.

Also in the Library is a games table, again of rosewood,

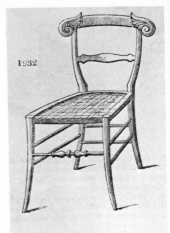

117 and 118 Designs for chairs published by J. C. Loudon in 1833. The chair in Fig. 119 incorporates features from them both.

119 Cane-seated chair of beechwood painted to simulate rosewood, made By Banting, France and Co., in about 1829. Height 81·3cm.

the frieze inlaid with brass and the shaped top fitted with a pierced brass gallery at the ends. It is referred to very briefly in the invoice as 'A rosewood Chess Table £14. 0. 0.' As can be seen in the illustration (Plate 9, page 119) the supports take the form of lyres, somewhat unconventionally placed upside down.

The chair in Fig. 119, is one of a large number of real or simulated rosewood chairs at Ickworth and in view of the bald description in the suppliers' invoices they cannot be identified with certainty. Their design can, however, be traced to J. C. Loudon's *Encyclopaedia*, a highly popular book first published in 1833 and reissued with various revisions during the ensuing 44 years. Loudon shows a number of 'fancy chairs for drawing rooms; they may be made of rosewood, maple, satin, or any other kind of fancy wood . . . the seats are first caned, and then covered in patterns with willow (split willow rods) of different colours, produced by staining, so as very successfully to imitate various kinds of woods'. Two of Loudon's chairs are illustrated in Figs 117 and 118, with the Ickworth painted beechwood chair beside them. It can be seen that the latter is a combination of the others: the criss-cross back is allied with the carved top-rail to produce a third design.

The foregoing is a clear example of the manner in which styles have been built up over the centuries, with motifs added and subtracted to produce variations and improvements. Looked back upon, there would seem to have been definite breaks as, for instance, when the Rococo was replaced by the Neo-classical, but in fact there was a very gradual transition from one to the other over a period of years. It was an endless process, and in the case of furniture the cabinet-maker played an important part. Although the designer was paramount, much depended on the judgment and skill of the actual craftsman making the piece, and English furniture owes just as much to the men who used chisels and other tools to such effect as it does to the creators and engravers of designs.

Bibliography

Thomas Chippendale, **The Gentleman and Cabinet-Maker's Director**, reprinted 1957

A. Coleridge, **Chippendale Furniture**, 1968

R. Edwards and M. Jourdain, **Georgian Cabinet-Makers**, 3rd edn, 1955

Furniture History, journal of the Furniture History Society, 1965 (in progress)

G. Eland (ed), **Purefoy Letters**, 2 volumes, 1931

C. Hayward, **Antique or Fake?**, 1970

H. Hayward (ed), **World Furniture**, 1965

C. F. Hummel, **With Hammer in Hand**, Charlottesville, Va, 1968

A. Heal, **London Furniture Makers 1660–1840**, 1953, reprinted 1972

W. Ince and J. Mayhew, **The Universal System of Household Furniture**, reprinted 1960

S. von La Roche, **Sophie in London, 1786**, trans C. Williams, 1933

J. C. Loudon, **Encyclopaedia of Cottage, Farm and Villa Architecture**, 1833, reprinted partially: **Loudon's Furniture Designs**, ed C. Gilbert, 1970

P. Macquoid and R. Edwards, **The Dictionary of English Furniture**, 2nd edn, revised by R. Edwards, 3 volumes, 1954

C. Musgrave, **Regency Furniture**, 1961

H. C. Smith, **Buckingham Palace**, 1931

J. T. Smith, **Nollekens and His Times**, ed W. Whitten, 2 volumes, 1920

R. W. Symonds, **Furniture-making in 17th and 18th Century England**, 1955

J. Toller, **Antique Miniature Furniture**, 1966

P. Ward-Jackson, **English Furniture Designs of the Eighteenth Century**, 1958

F. J. B. Watson, **Wallace Collection Catalogues: Furniture**, 1966

G. Wills, **English Furniture 1550–1760 and 1760–1900**, 2 volumes, 1971

Index

Bold figures refer to illustrations.